DON'T MAKE ME USE MY LIFE COACH VOICE

THE ART AND SCIENCE OF LIFE COACHING FOR NEWCOMERS

ELVIN COACHES

CONTENTS

Introduction   7

1. THE ESSENCE OF ENLIGHTENED   13
   COACHING
   Famous People Who Love Life Coaches   16
   So, What Can a Life Coach Do for You?   18
   Common Misconceptions of Life Coaches   24
   Why You Should Become a Life Coach   27
   Common Challenges of Life Coaching   30
   Keeping It Private   32

2. THE INTUITIVE COACH   33
   Benefits of Working With an Intuitive Life   35
   Coach
   Methods of an Intuitive Life Coach   37
   Law of Attraction   40

3. POWERFUL COACHING TECHNIQUES AND   44
   SKILLS
   The Techniques You Need for Great Coaching   46
   Techniques That Will Benefit Your Clients   47

4. THE TIME TRAVEL COACHING TECHNIQUE   55
   Techniques to Create More Impact   60
   Techniques Requiring More Skill   67
   Other Effective Techniques   69

5. TYPES OF COACHING STYLES   71
   The Coaching Approach   72

6. CHAPTER 5: GREAT QUESTIONS TO ASK WHEN COACHING SOMEONE — 83

Making a Transformation — 84

Open-Ended Questions — 89

More Tips for Asking the Appropriate Questions — 90

Some More Questions — 93

7. THE SCIENCE OF HABITS — 97

Habits and Their Formation — 98

When You're Finally Ready to Make a Change — 107

What's in a Day? Or 21? — 115

How a Life Coach Can Help With Habit Change — 116

Promoting a Habit Challenge — 118

8. THE MINDSET COACHING — 119

You Are Here to Do Extraordinary Things — 121

Who Can Use a Mindset Coach? — 124

How Does a Mindset Coach Help? — 126

The End of a Session — 131

9. BUSINESS COACHING — 133

You as a Business Coach — 136

Selling Yourself as a Business Coach — 138

The Biggest Obstacles for Successful Business Coaching — 141

Building Trust — 146

Conclusion — 151

References — 157

Just for you!

Scan the QR code to subscribe or follow the link
https://elvinlifecoaches.activehosted.com/f/3

You're going to receive the

Wheel of Life Coaching Technique

and other goodies

INTRODUCTION

"The great thing in the world is not so much in where we stand as in what direction we are moving."

— OLIVER WENDELL HOLMES

Picture a man wandering aimlessly on the road. He is going in a certain direction, but if you were to stop and ask him where, he would not be able to tell you. This is because he has no actual direction and will just go where the road leads. The man will not know if he has arrived where he's supposed to be because he never really knew where he was going. When he's hungry, he will eat. When he's thirsty, he will drink. When he's tired, he will sleep. He will respond to his physiological needs, but beyond this, his life will have no real meaning. He is just doing what is needed to exist.

Unfortunately, this is a metaphor for how so many people live. People wander aimlessly through life with no real direction. They have no goals or ambitions, and therefore never create the life they were meant to have. I want better for you because I know that you deserve it. We all deserve to live a fulfilling life as long as we are willing to work for it. You must develop direction in order to truly get where you want to be. To have direction, you must create solid goals, objectives, and pathways for how you want to get there.

This can be challenging for those who are not used to it. Many individuals have learned to retreat when life gets challenging. They have numerous problems and have no idea how to resolve them. The great thing is, you have the answers inside of you. That's right! With any problems that come your way, you have the ability to come up with a solution. You have the capability, just like anyone else, to figure out your true path and create a life that you desire.

Sometimes, we just need some guidance from an outside source. The answers are somewhere inside of us, but we cannot figure out how to find them. There can be many reasons for this, like past failures, disappointments, pain, trauma, abuse, and a wealth of other setbacks. These act as mental roadblocks, and my goal is to help you tear them all down. We can make this happen together through the art of life coaching.

Life coaching is an interesting field. Many people confuse it with counseling, but the objectives are quite different. With counselors or therapists, their goal is to find solutions for you while dealing with mental health disorders, whereas a life coach helps you figure out things for yourself. They don't tell you how to live your life, but help you determine the type of life you want to live. A life coach will provide you with clarity so you can see the answers to your problems right in front of you. From there, it is up to you to move in the right direction.

By reading through the chapters in this book, you will learn about the immense benefits of life coaching and how to become one yourself so you can assist others in finding their pathway towards a better life too. By the time you are done, you will have a detailed understanding of what life coaching is and the immense benefits it provides. This book will also cover different types of life coaches that exist, the various techniques and methodologies used in coaching practices, how to form positive habits, and effectively coaching those who need it.

If you have been feeling lost and uncertain about life, don't be too hard on yourself. It happens to everybody, but the key is to find the right solutions. This is what I am here to help you with through my book, *Don't Make Me Use My Life Coach Voice*. I understand the feeling of being lost and in pain. I know how it feels to not know where you're going. These feelings are not unusual, so never think yourself to be weird for having them.

However, you also cannot allow yourself to live this way forever. At some point, you must look towards greener pastures to find and create better circumstances. Otherwise, you will be stuck in an existence that you find miserable and restrictive. Once again, you have the power to get out of your rut because you know yourself the best. I am simply here to guide you. If you are ready to start your life coaching journey, come with me and I will show you how.

(David, n.d.)

WHO AM I?

Well, before you take my advice, I assume you would like to know more about me first. I am part of a group called Elvin Coaches, which is a collective of people who love to help and guide others towards a better life and circumstances. We all met each other during an event in Bali, Indonesia several years ago.

We were there to study the life coaching process and bonded with one another almost instantly. Over the years, we have become closer and now feel like a family.

Life coaching has become a passion for all of us, and we have collectively helped numerous individuals during our many years of training. Life coaching is not just a career or business at Elvin Coaches, but a passion and lifestyle by which we all swear by. This means that if we are not actively helping people, we feel an emptiness inside, as if there's a piece of us missing.

Because we are so passionate about life coaching, we wanted to impart our knowledge and training to you. We felt that the best way to reach the masses was by writing a book detailing our ideas. We want to help you, the reader, learn about life coaching so you can benefit from the practice and even become a life coach yourself someday if you choose. The information provided in this book, *Don't Make Me Use My Life Coach Voice,* helped all of us during some of the most challenging times in our lives, and we are confident it will help you too, just like it has for many other clients that have crossed our paths.

All of us at Elvin Coaches still experience the ups and downs of life. There are days when we are on top of the world, while others, we are down and out and just want to hide somewhere. Getting through life is a constant battle, and none of us will ever tell you differently. We do not promise that all of your problems will go away; however, you will be equipped with better tools to handle them. After learning the techniques used in life coaching, you will look at your life in a completely different way.

Ultimately, we want to help you find the solutions for your life and also guide you into becoming life coaches yourself. Once you learn to put yourself back together, you can help other people do the same. That is the mindset here at Elvin Coaches. We coached ourselves to become better people. Now, we will help you become coaches in the same manner.

All of us at Elvin Coaches want to thank you in advance for listening to our words. If you are ready to become the ultimate life coach, keep reading.

Team

1

THE ESSENCE OF ENLIGHTENED COACHING

Enlightenment

For those of you who are sports fans, I want you to think about your favorite athlete. If you are not a sports fan, think about an actor, singer, or any type of performer that you admire. How do these individuals make you feel when you watch them perform at their highest level? I imagine that it's a powerful experience for you. Now, I want you to realize that all of these individuals had someone behind the scenes to help hone their craft and provide motivation. In most cases, it was some type of coach. All great performers out there had some assistance in becoming who they are with their talents. Athletes have head coaches, defensive coaches, or offensive coaches. Other celebrities may have voice coaches, acting coaches, or speech coaches.

After understanding this, does it make their talents seem any less significant? Of course, it doesn't because all great men and women had some type of guidance throughout their lives. It might have been direct face-to-face coaching or learning from afar. Either way, everybody needs help, and getting it does not make them any less smart, talented, or skilled.

Since these entertainers have coaches for their careers, why would someone not consider having a coach for their lives? A life coach is someone who will help you live your best life. They will be a guiding light so you can make the best decisions for yourself. The art of life coaching provides a synergistic relationship between the coach and their client. Eventually, this will lead a person to tap into their full potential and live the life they were meant to have. So often, people are just existing rather than living. They are constantly falling short of where their talents can actually take them. It's time to change this routine and give your life new meaning.

If you are feeling lost or need to be pointed in the right direction, a life coach will help you grow out of this by analyzing your current situation, identifying your limiting beliefs, and customizing a plan to help you overcome any obstacles standing in your way. They can help you see the big picture and focus your mind on your desired goals.

The relationship a person has with their life coach is personal and professional at the same time. A life coach will learn a lot about you, but will also need to keep boundaries. They cannot be manipulated by emotions, so they must remain objective. Still, the partnership can be creative by targeting the help towards individual wants and needs. No one person is the same, so a good coach is able to identify the best ways to help different clients which are unique to that individual. Through their assistance, a client will be able to:

- Create a clear vision for themselves based on their specific goals in life.
- Modify goals, as needed, based on changes in circumstances.
- Discover more about themselves.
- Confront their fears and dark past if they have one.
- Develop a plan of action with concrete strategies for change.

A combination of all of these will lead to a more fulfilling life. When you start working with a life coach, you will understand the true value it brings. If you act as a life coach for others, you will understand how helping others allows you to grow yourself.

FAMOUS PEOPLE WHO LOVE LIFE COACHES

While we don't want you to do something simply because a celebrity does, the fact that so many famous people in their field attribute their success to life coaches is a testament to how beneficial the practice can be. It has boosted some careers and revitalized others. The following are some celebrities who credit life coaches with helping them immensely during their careers (Casano, 2016).

- Oprah Winfrey: She credits much of her success to her personal life coach, Martha Beck, and has been a major advocate of this practice for decades. She even suggests life coaches to members of her audience who may be struggling.
- Nia Long: She has been an actress for over 20 years and credits her life coach for helping her live a more fulfilling life.
- Danny Bonaduce: After his success in the highly popular series *The Partridge Family*, Mr. Bonaduce suffered immensely due to drug use, homelessness, and legal issues. After working with a life coach, he was able to become grounded again and get his life back on track. He loved life coaching so much that he eventually became one himself.
- Von Miller: He is the star linebacker for the Denver Broncos football team. Back in 2011 and 2013, he had

problems with the law. His entire career could have been over. Luckily, this did not happen to Mr. Miller. He sought out a life coach to help him turn his life around and has since become a Super Bowl champion and MVP.

- Metallica: Arguably one of the most famous bands of all time. After going through some heated feuds, the members received help from a life coach and were able to realign themselves with a common goal. They worked together in harmony to achieve great success.

- Leonardo DiCaprio: He has worked with probably the most famous and successful life coach of all time, Tony Robbins. While Mr. DiCaprio is silent about the work he did with Mr. Robbins, his immense movie success speaks for itself.

- Chuck Liddell: A highly successful MMA fighter and UFC legend, Mr. Liddell is both physically and mentally tough. During his prime, he was one of the best and most feared fighters in the world. Mr. Liddell actually worked with Tony Robbins at one point to help him strengthen the mental aspect of his game. This would complement his physical gifts pretty well, making him a lean, mean, fighting machine.

- Hugh Jackman: Mr. Jackman also worked with Tony Robbins, whom he had been seeking out for years. The specifics are not well known, but Mr. Jackman has nothing but praise for Mr. Robbins.

- Andre Agassi: One of the greatest tennis players of all time, Mr. Agassi credits the help of a life coach for taking him from the 126th to the number one tennis player during his time.
- Serena Williams: Probably the greatest female tennis player of all time, Ms. Williams also credits Tony Robbins for helping her with the success she has had. After battling injuries for years, she was stressed and worn out. When she worked with Mr. Robbins, she was able to persist and train through her injuries and eventually win a Grand Slam.

This is a truly versatile list of people, which showcases the effectiveness of life coaching. The practice can always be targeted towards an individual's needs, making them the best version of who they are. If you still discount the value of a good life coach, keep on reading. Well, keep on reading regardless.

SO, WHAT CAN A LIFE COACH DO FOR YOU?

Essentially, a person will work with a life coach because they want to have a better life tomorrow than they have today. They want to see growth in every area of their lives, including personal, professional, health, and relationships. A life coach can help you identify the gaps that exist between where you are and where you want to be. Once this happens, it will be your job to build the bridges and close the gaps.

When you are wondering about the necessity of life coaching, you're impeding yourself from unlocking an extraordinary life. Even the most successful among us can improve in some way. There is always something missing that we cannot find unless someone guides us in doing so. Having the talent and bird's-eye view of a life coach can help all of us find what is holding us back.

Your relationship with a life coach does not have to be short term. They can help and guide you throughout your life and struggles. You might be wondering right now what the difference is between a life coach and a friend. Well, a friend will have a personal connection with you, so they will provide advice from an area of subjectivity rather than objectivity. Furthermore, while a friend can provide advice, a trained life coach can help uncover a person's deepest thoughts to determine their strengths and weaknesses, and how they can improve upon both. There are a few key elements that make working with a life coach worth it.

Accountability

Most life coaches have a long-term relationship with their clients, as long as the chemistry is there. They will also have regularly scheduled phone calls or in-person meetings to assess their clients' progress. Essentially, if you are not making positive changes in your life, you will have to answer for them. A good life coach will not allow you to make excuses. If a plan was laid for success, you better believe you will be held accountable for following it.

Think of this as having a personal trainer while you're working out. You will push yourself much harder when you know someone is watching you. This is just human nature. The same goes for having a life coach. When you know someone will follow up with you and expect results, then you are more likely to work harder to achieve them.

"Integrity is doing the right thing, even when no one is looking."

— C.S. LEWIS

The above quote relates to people just doing what they're supposed to, even if no one is watching them. Unfortunately, people become lackadaisical when they think they're alone and no one is holding them accountable. Even the mildest pressure of knowing a life coach will be asking some tough questions is motivation enough for people to get in gear.

Expertise

Life coaches are trained and skilled in knowing how to help you come up with the right goals, improve your financial success, and better structure your personal life. With a coach like this on your side, you can significantly increase your success. Remember, Michael Jordan had Phil Jackson; Tom Brady had Bill Belichick; and Mike Tyson, at his best, had Kevin Rooney. Even top business professionals have someone advising them. Behind every successful person throughout history is a coach of some kind guiding them to be their best.

Delivery

While your friends and family members might mean well, they do not always know the right things to say. Their words can turn into lecturing or nagging, which is not helpful at all. A well-trained life coach knows exactly how to motivate their clients so they can be at their very best. The motivational words of a life coach are usually provided over the phone or some type of video call, like Skype or Zoom. In-person meetings happen too, but if a life coach lives in another area and has multiple clients, remote access is the best option and one they will likely choose.

Speed of Progress

Clients who work with life coaches often report that everything in their lives starts moving at rapid speed and much more efficiently. Again, having accountability plays a huge role. People are pushed to make actual changes, which means life will be improving in many ways. Even during uncomfortable times, forward progress is happening. In fact, during times of discomfort, the most positive changes are happening.

People seek out life coaches because they feel their lives have no meaning. Even if they're successful in one aspect, they could be lacking in many others. A life coach can point out how simple some solutions are, and how minor changes can ultimately lead to major success. When you decide to go down this path, dreams that were once out of reach can become a reality. Immediately after working with a life coach, you will find yourself changing and growing in many of the following ways:

- Taking more effective action steps. Remember that just because you're acting does not mean you are moving in the right direction.
- Ignoring petty annoyances that disrupt your day.
- Creating momentum in your life to achieve great results. Success can be addictive once you get a taste of it.
- Setting more affirmative goals based on what you actually want in life. This is because your clarity and focus are much better, and you will be able to define a vision for success.
- Identifying your limiting beliefs that have been holding you back.

In addition to these, there are many personal adjustments that may occur based on the individual. Some of these changes include:

- Increased financial stability resulting from better money management, starting a business, getting a promotion, or a combination of many things.
- Being able to maintain a work/life balance. Understanding which one needs your attention and what moment becomes essential.
- Learning to communicate more succinctly and effectively. Wasting words will no longer be a problem for you.
- Fostering more powerful connections professionally and personally
- Achieving weight loss and/or fitness goals
- Managing an important life or business transition

There are many different types of life coaches, and we will describe them in more detail throughout the different chapters in this book. Some coaches focus on well being and spirituality. Others are more professionally minded and do things like helping you get organized or take a left brained approach to improving your life. You can seek out specific types of coaches based on what your particular needs are.

While life coaching does not require a specific certification, there are many training programs out there that will provide you with the tools and certifications to make you a credible coach. The International Coach Federation (ICF) is a leading organization that provides independent certification and sets the professional standards by which life coaches should practice. Currently, life coaching is not a regulated profession.

COMMON MISCONCEPTIONS OF LIFE COACHES

Life coaches are talented and help make the lives of many people better through their efforts. In this section, we will clarify some of the misconceptions that exist so you can fully understand what you are getting into. Life coaching encompasses many different things, but there are also many things it is not.

Life Coaching Is Not Counseling or Therapy

Many individuals conflate life coaching by comparing the practice to psychology, psychiatry, or other form of therapy. While it can intertwine with these areas, it is not the same thing. A therapist is a licensed professional that helps individuals with current or past issues of the mind and helps them overcome trauma. Life coaches deal with a person's present circumstances and assist them in building a future.

Life coaches definitely do not treat mental health disorders or give any type of medical advice. If this becomes apparent during a session, the coach should immediately refer the client to a therapist if they are not already seeing one. Most life coaching clients are healthy and successful, but they feel stuck or want more from their lives. They want to grow personally and professionally.

While there was once a lot of tension between life coaches and therapists, mainly because therapists felt coaches were stepping on their toes by practicing without a license, the attitude has started to change. One of the reasons is the whole "practicing therapy without a license" is false. Second, therapists have adopted an "if you can't beat them, join them" attitude. Many have recognized the need for coaching and have transitioned into this practice themselves. If you are working with a practitioner of both, the relationship needs to be made clear in regard to what you need. The therapist/life coach also needs to be straightforward about what service they are providing so the client does not become confused.

Life Coaching Is a Real Profession

Many people see life coaching as a hobby or side hustle. However, it is a real career and passion. They are able to help many people improve their lives and can create a lot of business doing so. If you decide to become a life coach, think of yourself as your own business person.

Life Coaches Do Not Need Training

Life coaches do not need to be certified; however, if you want to have long-term success in the field, going through a good training program is essential. You must learn the appropriate methods and communication strategies that will be beneficial to your clients. Otherwise, you could lead them astray, overstep your boundaries, or just not be helpful in any way. Life coaching is not just about speaking and telling people what to do. You must also know what to say, when to say it, and how to make it effective. You must also be a great listener so you can determine your client's needs.

The general public also trusts coaches who have certification. They feel their help will be more appropriate and beneficial. In a survey done by the International Coaching Federation (ICF), 84% of coaching clients stated in the affirmative when asked whether or not they care if their life coaches are certified (Stewart, 2014). If you want a successful life coaching practice, getting certified will be a positive investment.

Not All Coaches Are Slimy

Because the profession is not currently regulated, anyone can put up a sign and call themselves a life coach. They don't go through any training, don't learn any of the skills, and are only in it for a cash grab. That being said, there are many fine, reputable, and highly trained coaches out there. You just have to do your research. Remember, there are unethical people in every profession. You cannot judge the whole field by a few bad apples.

Coaching Is for Everyone

Coaching first started catching on when movie stars, high-level executives, and billionaires began using them. Over the years, the effectiveness of life coaching has become apparent. Coaches now specialize in helping people through all walks of life, so no matter what position you are in, there is a life coach available to help you.

WHY YOU SHOULD BECOME A LIFE COACH

Coaching

Life coaching is a dynamic profession that continues to grow and prosper. With so many individuals realizing the benefits it can have for them, there are no real signs of slowing down. The reason for writing this book is not just to tell you about how life coaching can help you, but encourage you to become one yourself if you choose. If you have liked the information thus far, consider taking this on as a passion. It can benefit you, and others, in many significant ways. We will go more in depth into the different types of coaching and specific techniques a person can utilize. Before getting there, let's go over some reasons why life coaching might be a perfect fit for you.

.   .   .

You Love Helping People

Are you someone who is always helping people? Do people feel safe coming to you with their problems? Are you the go-to person to help resolve an issue? Are you a great listener who truly hears someone out before responding? If so, life coaching might be right up your alley. Life coaches contribute a lot to help people live better lives, and you will have the opportunity to do this if you follow down this path. As you help others, you will help yourself too. Life coaches learn a lot from their clients, as well.

You Need a Higher Purpose by Helping Others

Do you find yourself in a field that is not satisfying to you? Are you just going through the motions to get a paycheck? Do you have a desire to serve other people? Life coaching gives you a great opportunity to serve others, which will also give you a higher purpose in life. Not only that, once your clientele grows, you can replace the income of a job that gives you no meaning.

You Help People Line up With Their Values

One of the things coaches help their clients with is to recall and understand their true values and beliefs in life. From there, they can help the client set up their goals according to these values. Imagine being able to help someone figure out their life's work. This can become a reality for you as a life coach.

. . .

You Value Time and Freedom

The great thing about life coaching is that you can do it from anywhere and at any time. You can have clients from all over the world and help them out over the phone or during a video conference call. You can assist one of your clients in the morning at your local coffee shop, then have a Skype call with someone in the afternoon that lives in another country. You can even talk to clients while you're vacationing on a cruise or staying at a resort by the beach. With life coaching, you will have the time and freedom to work when you want and where you want. Trade in that nine-to-five structured lifestyle and become an independent coach while helping so many people. You will be your own boss and won't have to answer to anyone.

Don't Do It for the Money

I am going to be upfront with you. Life coaching has the potential to bring in a lot of money. Some of the top coaches out there charge hundreds of dollars per hour. I am not guaranteeing these wages, but it's certainly possible. I don't want your focus to be on the money, though. Pay attention to your clients' needs, build relationships, and help as many people as you can, and eventually the finances will start flowing in.

Now that we have provided a general overview of what life coaching is, we will get into some more specific topics.

COMMON CHALLENGES OF LIFE COACHING

I admit we are a little biased here at Elvin Coaches because we love the life coaching profession. We have seen with our own eyes the many people who have changed their lives after getting the help of a great coach. The practice is valuable and we understand that. We all hope that you do too. That being said, this section will be dedicated to some of the challenges related to life coaching. These are not meant to be a deterrent. Our hope is that you will go into life coaching as a profession and a passion. We just want you to be fully informed before making the dive. This is something we would do during a coaching session and will make sure we do it here, as well.

- Building a trusting relationship. Before dismissing your client as uncoachable, determine if you've done enough to build a relationship where they trust you. Trust is essential for a good coach and client interaction.
- Avoid doing the heavy lifting. Your job as a coach is to ask the right questions and help your clients seek out answers. If they aren't coming up with solutions on their own, do not jump in, no matter how tempting it is. That is not your job as a coach. Keep asking follow-up questions until you get somewhere.
- Making your client reliant on you. Once again, this happens when you solve their problems for them.

They need to do it on their own. You do not want your client to become reliant on you. You actually want them to need you as little as possible, as crazy as that may sound.

- Having a client who thinks they know everything is a major issue. It can make the coach feel like they're obsolete. Arrogant people like this are not coachable. Arrogant people need to be challenged with some tough questions that make them open up more. If they continue to dismiss your help, you can only go so far. Save your energy for someone who will appreciate you.

- Clients can sometimes refuse to take action. Successful coaching is about giving accountability to the person being coached. If they are unwilling to set goals and take the proper steps, you can explore new goals with them, push them to make a commitment, or eventually break ties if none of the above work.

Life coaching definitely has its challenges, and some clients will be harder to break through than others. However, when you are dealing with a challenging situation with a client who is at the lowest point in their lives, watching them turn around and pick themselves back up is one of the greatest highs you will receive.

KEEPING IT PRIVATE

Security

A major theme throughout this book will be the idea of trust. Trust is extremely important in a coach-client relationship, and without it, no progress will be made. As a life coach, your client will reveal things about themselves that their best friends and closest family members may not know. They trust you with this information, and you need to take this very seriously.

Even though you are not expected to deal with medical issues, you must handle what your clients tell you in the same manner as protected health information. Therefore, everything they tell you must stay between the coach and the client. Respecting privacy is essential. If you don't, all trust will be lost, and rightfully so.

2

THE INTUITIVE COACH

"Intuition is always right in at least two ways; It is always in response to something. It always has your best interest at heart."

— GAVIN DE BECKER

W e all have intuition, which can also be called a gut feeling. It is the ability to understand or feel something immediately, without the need for conscious reasoning, like when you are about to walk down a certain street but get an uncomfortable vibe about it. It is important to listen to our intuition because it is trying to tell us something our conscious mind may not be aware of.

An intuitive life coach is someone who can guide you on the right path and reach your goals by helping you access your intuition. This part of your psyche knows a lot about you, and you will learn a lot about yourself by paying attention to it. The ultimate objective of an intuitive coach is the same as any regular coach; they just have some different strategies. In addition to the secular elements of life, like habits, mind blocks, goal-setting, and action steps, they also bring in some spiritual principles into their practice so you can tap into your divine energy. This is to help you connect with the deepest parts of yourself, which you may have never even been aware of.

During your sessions with an intuitive coach, you can expect to be challenged to confront the issues that have been holding you back your whole life. Clients who are not used to this can become very uncomfortable during these moments. Confronting your limiting beliefs is never easy, but absolutely necessary if you want to heal. Once you are able to do this, you will fully recognize your strengths, weaknesses, and various issues you need to overcome. This can provide much guidance as you follow the path to living the life of your dreams.

An intuitive coach will generally work with the energy you give off. This will help them guide you in resolving your deepest issues. The energy you are projecting is coming from your intuition, which will let the coach know what your blockages are. After this, they can assist you in developing new thoughts, habits, and beliefs that support the life you really want and not the one you are pretending to love. Once you are past these issues, you can open yourself up to all of the opportunities that exist for you. Life has so much to offer all of us, and the intuitive life coach can help us realize that.

BENEFITS OF WORKING WITH AN INTUITIVE LIFE COACH

After working with an intuitive life coach, you will be able to adjust your thoughts and feelings so that they vibrate at a frequency that matches your desired life. We are all filled with thoughts that can sabotage our lives, and we don't even realize it. However, thoughts lead to actions, and actions lead to results. So, if our thoughts are limiting, our results will be too. If our thoughts are destructive, our results will be too. The proper life coach can help you nip them in the bud.

Through intuitive life coaching, you will get to know yourself better on a spiritual level. This does not mean you will start following a certain religion or deity. Of course, that could end up being the case. However, spirituality goes well beyond religion and has a much deeper meaning for most people. There are so many things you can get out of intuitive life coaching, like finding your purpose in life, discovering your dream career, healing past relationships, and learning what you really want in life. Perhaps you have been stuck in your hometown and determine you need to leave. This might be the place where all of your painful memories exist, and an intuitive life coach can help you figure it out. The following are a few other things that can happen for you while working under an intuitive life coach:

- Develop a new passion in life that you never even knew you were interested in.
- Take up some new hobbies that give meaning to your life. Some of these can even turn into a new career path.
- Achieve financial abundance by tapping into an unknown skill.
- Start a new business based on your passion.
- Become healthier and happier as a person.
- Discover how to listen more to your intuition.
- Live a better life overall.

You will receive a tremendous amount of benefits from intuitive life coaching, many of which you won't even realize until you go through it. You will be amazed at how much you learn about yourself. If you are unsure if you need help this type of life coach, do a self-assessment and determine if you have any of these feelings on a regular basis:

- Anger
- Resentment
- Unfulfillment
- Shame
- Depression

- Emptiness
- Jealousy
- Loneliness
- Lack of motivation
- Confusion

While everyone has these emotions at some point in their lives, they should never dominate your psyche. If they do, major changes need to be made. It might be time to work with an intuitive life coach, who can work on improving your self-love, confidence, and worldview.

METHODS OF AN INTUITIVE LIFE COACH

While intuitive life coaches are not medical practitioners, they do possess their own methods of healing that are beneficial to anybody. There can be many reasons why a person would need healing, including past trauma, dysfunctional relationships, bad career choices, or poor self-care. The focus of their practices is holistic techniques to help rebuild the body and mind. The methods can include:

- Hypnotherapy: This is when hypnosis is done for therapeutic purposes and helps clients initiate change on the subconscious level.
- Crystal healing: The use of crystals and gemstones to

absorb negative energy and replace it with positive energy.

- Reiki: A touch healing method that originates from Japan. The practitioner manipulates and channels energy into the client's body to create a balance within the body and mind.
- Chakra healing: This originates from India and is based on the idea that humans have a number of energy fields, known as chakras, which relate to different portions of the body. The knowledge of these energetic centers is used to establish balance and harmony.

While all of these practices are a part of intuitive life coaching, it is not a necessity for the field. A person's intuition can be accessed without these specific healing techniques. However, if you plan on becoming an intuitive life coach, consider learning these methods for effective energy manipulation. If you end up going down this path, you will be able to help people with their relationships, career, health, passion, self-love, confidence, creativity, spirituality, and pretty much every aspect of their lives.

Still Not Therapy

When we talk about intuitive life coaches being healers, people will assume that they're therapists. However, as we mentioned earlier, life coaches are not therapists in any way because they cannot diagnose illnesses or deal with any pathologies of the mind. The healing practices are centered around improving energy and are not related to clinical healing. If an intuitive life coach ever feels like they're dealing with significant mental disorders, they should be referring their clients to a licensed practitioner of therapy.

In addition to not treating specific disorders, an intuitive life coach will never tell you what to do with your life. That is not for them to decide, but they will help guide you in making your own decisions. An intuitive coach will also motivate you, but never force you to make changes or aggressively push you into taking action steps. Once again, that is up to you. Finally, they will not predict your circumstances. The future is uncertain and none of us know what will truly happen. However, we can set ourselves up as much as we can to build our lives as we desire.

LAW OF ATTRACTION

The basis of the Law of Attraction is that what we put out into the universe is what we ultimately attract. Our thoughts put out our specific energy, and that energy comes back to us in a similar fashion. For example, if we are thinking about excess wealth, good health, and positive relationships, the universe will hear this and we will have an abundance of these in our lives. Even if we are thinking about something in the negative, like if we are thinking about not living in poverty, we will still attract it because it is in our minds and therefore that's the energy we are putting out.

Negative emotions send off negative vibrations. Emotions like sadness, anger, shame, or hatred will snowball, and you will create more of these within yourself. On the other hand, positive emotions will do the same thing. Therefore, if you are happy, peaceful, and motivated, the vibrations you give off will attract more of these emotions.

Many intuitive life coaches subscribe to the idea of the Law of Attraction. They can help their clients change their thoughts from negative to positive, so they only attract more of these later on. In this manner, they are using the Law of Attraction to their advantage.

While people don't deserve bad things to happen to them because they are thinking negatively, it certainly is an explanation of why unhealthy emotions beget further unhealthy emotions.

The Law of Attraction can be targeted toward any area of your life, whether money, career, relationships, or success. The Universe is much smarter than we give it credit for, and if you want it to be on your side, give it some good vibes. This particular law does not discriminate based on age, race, gender, or cultural background. Simply put, what you focus on is what you will get. It may not happen right away, but ultimately, as the mind thinketh, the universe giveth.

In some form or another, the Law of Attraction has existed for centuries. Most of the major religions, like Christianity, Judaism, or Buddhism, have incorporated the philosophy into their teachings. Hence, this is not a new phenomenon. While the exact mechanism is not fully understood, many scientists such as quantum physicists have given more insight into the scientific basis of the law. As individuals, we do not have to understand the details; we just have to recognize how the law works. Once we do, our life will be filled with abundance.

To clear things up a little bit, the Law of Attraction is not some type of magic wand. It does not mean that if you imagine a pile of money, hundred-dollar bills will start falling from the sky. However, if your focus is on financial wealth, the universe will present more opportunities to make money.

Now that you understand the law, start making it work for you. Transition your thoughts so you stop thinking about all of the negative things in life. Instead, paint a picture in your mind about your ideal circumstances. Be specific about where you want to live, the friends you want around you, and the career you want to have. Use real-life visuals, like pictures, positive quotes written down, or screensavers on your computer to keep these positive images in your mind.

Once your thoughts automatically veer towards the positive, you will eventually have an abundance of things you want. It really is that simple, but it won't be easy. It takes constant effort to steer your mind away from negative thinking, but once you are living your dream life, it will all be worth it. Once again, work with an intuitive life coach that can help you with the Law of Attraction.

If you are someone who enjoys working with energy and believes in the power of intuition, consider going down this career path. Just like with general coaching, you will be able to make a difference in so many people's lives and use your own unique talents for healing purposes. You will also have the time and freedom to work from anywhere at any time you want.

In the next chapter, we will get into more coaching techniques that are powerful, effective, and elicit change.

3

POWERFUL COACHING TECHNIQUES AND SKILLS

Ideas!

While any average Joe can stake out a location and call themselves a life coach, they will ultimately get exposed for the frauds that they are. We just hope too many people do not get harmed in the process. The bottom line is, life coaching takes a certain amount of skill and talent in order to perform effectively. A person must also have the right mindset, which is to help people. This can also be developed over time, but is beneficial to have as the reason for going into this field.

The focus of this chapter will be the proper techniques and skills needed to be a great life coach. There are reasons why Tony Robbins, John Maxwell, Wayne Dyer, and Brian Tracy get a lot of clients. They utilize techniques that are effective and well-respected. Many people, including those at the top of their field, seek out these professionals to help them in the darkest moments of their lives. We mentioned several of the celebrities in the previous chapter who relied on the help of life coaches during their dark periods.

Life coaching is a serious practice that is gaining more steam every day. When you become a life coach, I want you to realize that people will put a lot of their faith and trust into you. I hope that you take this trust very seriously. I hope you take the life coaching profession, as a whole, very seriously and receive the proper training that you will need.

THE TECHNIQUES YOU NEED FOR GREAT COACHING

"The only difference between the master and the novice is that the master has failed more times than the novice has tried."

— STEPHEN MCCRANIE

Mastering anything in life does not happen overnight. It takes years of continuous practice to become a master, and once you get to that level, there is still more to learn. The point here is, life coaching will take time to master. In fact, you may practice this art for many years and still not master it. You may become good, even great, but that still won't make you a master. The objective is to never stop learning and growing. Also, never believe you know it all because trust me, none of us do.

As a life coach, you will have to make time to hone your skills, have the patience to never give up, and practice incessantly. Finally, you will need to work on mastering specific coaching techniques. Once you do, they will become your best friend and greatest resource. You cannot function as a life coach without some baseline methods. Even though you will become more creative and individualize techniques based on the client's needs, you still need a foundation to keep you grounded. In the end, this will be the ultimate deciding factor for your success. All of the other factors are just icing on the cake.

TECHNIQUES THAT WILL BENEFIT YOUR CLIENTS

There are numerous coaching techniques that a life coach will have at their disposal. If you get training at various academies for this field, you will probably learn different techniques. Many of these will have varying names, but the same course of action. I will go over some effective coaching techniques in this section that you can benefit from yourself, then use on clients when you get to that point.

The Wheel of Life Coaching Technique

The objective of this practice is to help a client take an honest, non-judgmental look at their current circumstances in life and focus on their most important areas. No matter how much discipline a person has, life continues to change and evolve, which causes them to stop paying attention to the important areas of their life. Priorities grow, change, and evolve constantly, and this can cause life to get away from a person. After a while, issues that are not vital to our lives and that we don't want anything to do with take up most of our time. The Wheel of Life coaching technique will help your client gain or regain a sense of direction, purpose, and balance. They will, once again, realize what really matters to them in life.

To begin using this technique, use the following steps:

- Ask your client to draw a regular circle on a piece of paper.
- Divide the circle into eight sections, like a pizza or a pie. Then label each section the following:
- Family and friends
- Romance
- Personal growth
- Business/career
- Finances
- Health
- Fun and recreation
- Physical environment
- Now, ask the client to label each section on a scale of one to 10, based on their satisfaction level. If they put zero, they are not satisfied at all. Write these numbers down on each separate segment.
- Once they have these items ranked, ask the client to start with the weakest areas of their lives, according to their own assessment, and come up with about three ways to boost each category. For example, if romance is a weak point, perhaps they can set aside 30 minutes every night and dedicate it to their spouse or partner if they have one.

The wheel of life provides a visual of a client's current reality and dream reality. Not only that, but it also forces them to come up with action steps to reach their desired life. If a client feels a lack of balance in their lives, this tool will help identify where the imbalance is. For instance, your career might be going perfectly, but your health and relationships might be suffering.

Popular motivational speaker and author Larry Winget heavily criticizes people who do not have a written plan for every area of their lives. This is why their work, health, relationships, and mind suffer continuously. When Mr. Winget is asked why people are poor, unhealthy, and miserable, his answer usually goes along the lines of, "Because they choose to be." You have to choose a better life by focusing on all areas. As he said, have a written down plan for all of these areas. The wheel chart can be your plan.

This tool does not have to be limited to eight sections. You can break it down even further. Also, you can create a wheel chart for specific areas of your life. For example, you can focus on your career or business and break it down into different areas that need to be addressed. This type of strategy should be done whenever you feel your life is not going in the proper direction.

The Moonshot Coaching Technique

Moonshot

Many individuals feel trapped in a routine that is meaningless, but they keep doing it on a daily basis because they feel like they can't do anything else. Also, it is easy to live this way because they don't have to evolve or challenge themselves in any way. They can simply live mindlessly and perform the same mundane practices day after day and year after year.

We've got some news for you. This is not really living, and if you decide to create your life this way, you will never grow, prosper, or create the life you have always wanted. You might as well be living as a zombie at this point.

"Don't live the same year 75 times and call it a life."

— ROBIN SHARMA

The Moonshot coaching technique is perfect for those clients who have lost their sense of adventure and excitement for life. People in this category would never live their lives off the cuff, even for a day. They would rather wake up and live the same boring existence from the day before with as little unpredictability as possible. As a life coach, your job is to help these individuals get out of the funk they are in. Help them realize once again how exciting life can be and how one day does not have to match the rest.

To perform this effective technique, take the following steps:

- Ask your client a series of challenging and unorthodox questions to get them out of their current mindset. Some examples include:
- What is a common dream that you always have?
- Are you ever jealous of what those around you are doing?
- What things excite you about life?
- If money was not an issue, what would be doing right now?
- Once they have answered these questions, have them

create a list of things they would love to be, have, and do. Don't limit them on what they can write down. Allow their imaginations to run free. Do they want to go to Mars? If so, they need to write it down. These are known as Moonshot Goals.

- After making their list, ask them to pick their top three which are big, but completely attainable.
- Work with your client to break down each goal into smaller and achievable steps. This will make the goal seem less daunting.

After practicing these strategies, the client should have a new thought process about how to live life. They will start changing their routines and be okay with challenging themselves. When a person gets out of their comfort zone, real growth starts to occur.

The Spheres of Influence Coaching Technique

There are many people who can't get a hold of their lives simply because they are overwhelmed with so many things. They become helpless and unsure of where to go or what to do. As a result, they spend an exorbitant amount of time and energy trying to work through problems, situations, and challenges they have no control over. They might not realize their lack of control because there is too much going on to remain focused. With the Sphere of Influence coaching technique, your client will realize that there are things they cannot control, so they should not waste energy doing so, and they should rather focus their attention on things they can control and influence.

Once individuals follow this technique, they will gain a lot of insight into what to walk away from. They will realize that the world's problems are not theirs to take on. To start implementing this technique, use the following steps:

- Have your client draw a large circle and then a smaller circle inside of it.
- In the smallest circle, have them write, "Things I can control." In the space between the large and small circle, have them write, "Things I can influence." Finally, outside of the large circle, have them write, "Everything else."
- Now, walk them through the individual challenges that they are struggling with. What is causing them to feel overwhelmed?
- As they are listing their problems, help them determine which part of the drawing each specific one needs to go into. For example, if a person is worried about losing their job, they can list the reason for their anxiety and worry in the following fashion.
- Things they can't control: The state of the economy, such as if the company is downsizing.
- Things they can influence: Developing better communication with their boss to determine what they

need to do to keep their job. This does not mean
kissing up or stooging on other employees.

- Things they can control: Building up their resume,
  searching for new jobs just in case, and reaching out to
  their network for possible opportunities.

This coaching technique will give your clients a clear view of
any situation. They will realize what they can and can't control
or influence, and therefore will become less overwhelmed and
more focused. They will have a sense of perspective to come up
with new ideas for growth and opportunities.

4

THE TIME TRAVEL COACHING TECHNIQUE

(GRUSHNIKOV, N.D.)

We are not talking about real time travel here. At least, not yet. However, we are talking about looking into the future. Many people have not taken steps to build the life they want because they are anxious about what will happen if they do. As a result, people are stuck in dead-end jobs because they can't bear the possibility of not having an income, remain in toxic relationships because they are worried about not having friends, or don't travel to a place they've always wanted to go because they are terrified of what might happen to them.

With the Time Travel coaching technique, you will guide your client in traveling to the future in an imaginary world and envision what their life could be like if they followed their dreams. To use this technique:

- Have your clients picture themselves in the future, anywhere from a few months to 10 years down the line. Then ask them some specific questions:
- What does your life look like? What do you see and hear? What does your daily routine look like from start to finish? Where do they live?
- Ask them if their imaginary picture is vastly different from what they have.
- Help them come up with smaller goals to attain the big picture goal they have in their mind.

This technique will help a client build some clarity around their values, desires, and goals.

∾

The Eisenhower Matrix Coaching Technique

Some major obstacles to success are prioritizations, time management, and productivity. All of these factors tie in to each other. They ultimately result in how well and efficiently you are able to complete something. No matter what you decide to do in life, whether it's entrepreneurship, working for a company, or being a stay-at-home parent, you will need to be able to handle things in a timely manner. Even your health and relationships can be affected by poor time management, productivity, and prioritization. For example, if your family is not getting an adequate amount of your attention, they might grow to resent you.

Before you can use the Eisenhower Matrix coaching technique, you must explain to your clients the difference between urgent and important.

- Urgent: This is anything that requires immediate attention. These situations generally don't have time to wait and put people into a reactive and defensive state. Urgent issues are generally tasks related to other people's goals.
- Important: This is anything that contributes to long-term gains. These types of issues put people in a responsive state where they have a sense of control and clarity.

Urgency!

After defining these terms, get out a piece of paper and draw a matrix, which should be one large square with four smaller quadrants inside of it. On the outer edges of the square, write 'urgent' above the first quadrant and 'important' to the left of it. Write "not urgent" above the second quadrant. For the third quadrant, write "not important" on the outside of it to the left. After this, label the inside of each quadrant the following:

- Quadrant 1: Do
- Quadrant 2: Plan
- Quadrant 3: Delegate
- Quadrant 4: Eliminate

Once the full matrix has been drawn, you will now have the client fill in the necessary information.

- Quadrant 1: Urgent and important issues. These can include things like getting an important project done for work, a major repair done on your home, or picking up the medications that you ran out of from the pharmacy.

- Quadrant 2: These are not urgent, but important tasks. These can be activities like going to the bank, buying groceries for the week, or calling a friend back who left you a message.
- Quadrant 3: These are urgent and not important. This might sound like an oxymoron, but hear us out. These are tasks that need to be quick but don't really carry a lot of weight, for example attending work meetings or replying to emails.
- Quadrant 4: These are not urgent or important tasks, for example scrolling through social media, playing video games, and watching TV.

After establishing what each quadrant is in detail, it is now time to prioritize them.

- Quadrant 1 tasks need to be done now with no delays.
- Quadrant 2 tasks can be planned for later on.
- Quadrant 3 tasks can probably be delegated.
- Quadrant 4 tasks can be deleted completely. Only do these after the first three quadrants are taken care of.

When you create and follow this grid, you will know what activities in your life require the most amount of attention.

From here, you will have much more clarity about what your goals should be.

All of these coaching techniques are effective in their own way and are the solutions for different problems a person might have. You may end up using one or a combination of all of these methods to help your client out. It's great to practice and be aware of all of these strategies because you never know when you might use them.

TECHNIQUES TO CREATE MORE IMPACT

We will go over some more impactful coaching techniques that will really start a mindset shift for your clients. You will really start seeing a transformation within your clients and how they view the world. There are four specific techniques with a simple strategy, but powerful results.

Technique 1

The first technique is called "The Perfect Day Exercise." Many clients live the same day over and over again and don't realize they can have something better. They can live a more purposeful life. As many of us get older, we forget how to daydream like we once did. As children, you might have been told to stop daydreaming and get back to reality. We are giving you permission to start doing this again, and tell your clients to do the same thing.

During the daydreaming phase, we are often imaging what our ideal life will be like. Of course, when we are five or six, we picture ourselves as superheroes, dinosaurs, or other mythical figures. As we get older, we start imagining what our perfect life will consist of. In many cases, the influential adults in our lives tell us to take a structured path filled with certainty and security. While these adults had our best interest at heart, they also severely limited our potential. As the years went by, we forgot our true dreams and desires, and instead focused on making a living.

The perfect day exercise gets us back into daydreaming and picturing what our ideal or perfect day looks like. When you have your clients practice this technique, have them write down in detail what they want to do throughout the day. What kind of career will they have? How early do they want to get up each day? At what time will their workday end? How many hours a day will they spend with family? What types of hobbies will they have? Where is their ideal place to live? These and many more questions should be answered by your client. You want them to be as detailed as possible.

Writing it down can help them visualize and remember their perfect day.

The goal of this exercise is not just to figure out what they want their lives to be like, but to help them realize the mindset shift that needs to occur. Finally, ask your client what is holding them back. You might be surprised by their responses, and they will be too. This final question can significantly change how your client approaches their work and daily routines. Instead of just existing, they may start living with the intent of changing.

You will be amazed at the perfect life your clients come up with and how they can be vastly different from their reality. For example, an unassuming accountant with a nine-to-five schedule might have a passion for music and the dream of being a guitar player. The perfect day exercise can give you a lot of surprises and can be a fun technique to employ.

Technique 2

The second technique involves using a coaching journal. It is estimated that the human mind has about 60,000 to 80,000 thoughts in a single day (Mindvalley, n.d.). Broken down, that's about 40-55 thoughts in a minute, so our minds are being inundated every moment of the day. It's impossible to recall all of these thoughts. In fact, most people forget them immediately and never pay attention to them again. The issue is, many of these thoughts could have given us deep insights about ourselves and the world we live in. The mind may have been trying to tell us something on the subconscious level, as well.

Having a coaching journal allows a person to keep their thoughts straight and recollect them later on. It is hard to process everything in our psyche in real time. Therefore, if you journal your thoughts throughout the day, you can revisit them any time and see where your mind wandered to.

As a coach, having your client utilize this technique can help all parties understand their true feelings. Our emotions in real time give us deep insight into what we want out of life. They can even give us a clue as to what we find repulsive. For example, if your client started feeling angry or depressed out of nowhere, he or she may not recognize it when it happened, but can look back on their journal and find out that these feelings occurred while they were around a certain group of people. On the other hand, if the person was extremely happy at a certain point, they can determine what was making them feel that way at that moment.

Ask your client to share their journal with you during the sessions. You can help them decipher what is going on and see if there is a pattern of thoughts that need to be addressed. Journaling is a powerful technique. Your clients can carry around a small notepad or even use a program on their phones. We realize it is not realistic to be journaling at every moment of the day, but have them do it whenever they get some downtime to recollect their emotions.

Technique 3

Check-in

At the beginning of each coaching session, you need to have a check-in with your client, and at the end of the session, you must have a check-out. These strategies can determine how well your interactions will go on any particular day. Many coaches ignore these practices, but they are essential for a positive session. The check-ins allow your client to drop any baggage from the outside world so they can be fully present during the coaching session. They can mention and then let go of any anger, anxiety, frustration, depression, and other negative emotions they might be carrying around. The coach is able to gauge where the client is coming from at this point, and they will both have a greater understanding during their interaction.

For the check-out, the coach and client will determine what action steps need to be taken to create some actual changes. While a client can leave a session feeling very motivated, it can go away really quickly once life starts to happen. Suddenly, everything that was gone over during the coaching session is gone forever and it will be back to square one again. A good check-out moment will allow the coach to see how effective the session was and how likely the client is to take real action. Having concrete steps to be held accountable for can make a client more likely to use the information they gained from a life coach. As a coach, you can also have certain goals and milestones that need to be completed by the next session.

Never skip the check-in and check-out. Take these moments to pause and make sure you are on the same page as your client.

Check-out

Technique 4

The final technique here is called the "what scares me?" technique. This process is pretty simple. Have your client write down all of their fears. Have them dig deep down and not just focus on superficial fears, like being afraid of the dark or spiders. Ask them what scares them at their core, like having a fear of failure, being alone, or letting their family down. What truly terrifies them in life to the point it becomes crippling?

Once you determine their fears, you can assess how much of their life is driven by them. Many of these exist on the subconscious level and are rooted in something mysterious, like a past trauma. Once the client's list is done, tackle each fear one at a time.

These techniques are effective for your coaching sessions, and you will make real progress with your clients. Once you begin mastering these skills, your clients will benefit a lot from you, and you will become a highly sought out coach in your field.

TECHNIQUES REQUIRING MORE SKILL

There are certain advanced techniques that some coaches will use, either because they were involved in a different field before coaching and had these skills beforehand, or they learned them to complement their coaching strategy. Whatever the case, you are not required to have these skills, but can choose to learn them if you want. I will go over these techniques to give you an idea of what they're about. From here, you can choose to incorporate them into your sessions or not. I will say that training in these methods can help you become more empowered as a life coach and help resolve more problem areas for your client.

Neuro-Linguistic Programming

This is a psychological approach used by individuals that involves analyzing, and eventually applying, strategies of successful people. As a life coach, you can use neuro-linguistic programming to help clients change their language and behavior techniques. Once they start mimicking the habits of successful people, they will start realizing their full potential.

Emotional Freedom Technique

Emotional freedom technique (EFT) is a form of acupuncture that does not use needles. Instead, the fingertips are used to access and stimulate the various energy points on the body. EFT is a great New Age method for dispelling excess emotional pain.

As a coach, you can also train in hypnotherapy to reach your patient while they are in a more relaxed state of being. From here, you can help your client become more motivated in breaking poor behavioral and cognitive patterns.

You will find that some of your clients have a very hard time expressing their feelings verbally. In these cases, you can have them perform writing exercises. Many people find it easier to be more clear and honest while writing than they are with speaking.

Cognitive Behavioral Coaching

This is not the same as cognitive behavioral therapy, which requires more of a psychological approach, similar to psychotherapy. Cognitive behavioral coaching is more about looking at a client's present thoughts and trying to improve them for the future. Basically, a coach will assist in replacing negative thought patterns with positive ones. As a coach, you will not be dealing with dysfunctions or mental health disorders. If this is necessary, you may have to refer your client to a licensed therapist.

Guided Meditation

Meditation is a truly powerful exercise that can help people become more mindful and less stressed, as well as reducing mental blocks. There are many books, classes, and practitioners that teach proper meditation techniques. You can even watch videos on YouTube to learn some simple methods. It can take years for people to master meditation practices, so learning the basics is good enough for your sessions. As a coach, you can guide your clients through meditation until they can do it on their own.

OTHER EFFECTIVE TECHNIQUES

I will end this chapter by going over some other effective techniques a coach can use during their sessions. These are also simple but work well.

Evidence Hunting

This is when you hunt for evidence throughout your life that shows the possibility of success in the future. A coach can help their client look for this evidence.

Perspective Change

The way a person experiences life has a lot to do with how they perceive things. Sometimes, the items we overly focus on can make our lives seem much grimmer than they actually are. Changing our perspective will bring new thoughts, which can give us a completely different outcome. As humans, we have a tendency to look at the negative side of everything, but a life coach can help us to refocus on the better parts of less favorable experiences and help us learn from them. This does not mean you are ignoring reality, just choosing to pay attention to the positive aspects of it.

Positive Affirmations

Positive affirmations are a way to reinforce your beliefs with more confidence and thus remove many negative internalized beliefs. We often have preconceived limitations on what we can handle. Affirmations like these can help back us up in times of belief crisis. A good life coach can help their clients come up with affirmations related to their goals and values.

All of these coaching techniques are powerful in their own way. Your clients will benefit from them greatly as they help solve their own unique problems. That best part is, they truly help coached clients find hidden answers within themselves.

TYPES OF COACHING STYLES

There is more than one way to skin a cat. There is always more than one route to get to a destination. If the door closes, go through a window. There are countless phrases and expressions out there to state the fact that there is no one way to do something. We all have our own styles that work best for us. This includes our coaching style. Despite following certain foundational rules, every life coach has their own personality. Some are more outspoken and aggressive, while others are soft-spoken and reserved.

As you come into your own as a coach, it is up to you what kind of style you utilize. Keep in mind that how your client takes you is important too. Different demeanors work better with various individuals and situations. You might have to change up your style every so often, and even within the same session, based on the progress you are making. The style you choose will have a remarkable impact on how your clients embrace your help. If they do not appreciate an aggressive approach, you must scale back and try something new. Being able to change up your methods is the only way to become a well-rounded life coach.

How you approach any coaching situation can literally make or break the rapport you have with a client. Your ultimate objective is to help them. Therefore, you must know how to gauge a situation well. The focus of this chapter will be the various coaching styles that exist and how they will work in various situations. Mastering the various coaching styles will make you an authority in the field and show your expertise to your clients. They will have more trust in you when they see that you have the ability to be flexible and change things up when needed. Confidence is attractive in a person, and whoever you work with as a coach will find you much more appealing in this regard.

Remember that a person is much more likely to take advice from someone who has their own life together. If you are scatter-brained, disorganized, and don't have anything in order, your clients will sense it immediately, and the relationship will become strained before eventually coming to an end.

THE COACHING APPROACH

Coaching styles are simply the social approaches and behavioral models that a life coach of any kind depends on for their personal brand and client needs. Some coaches develop a more authoritarian persona, while others create a friendly persona for themselves. Always understand that your reputation will precede you as a coach, so having multiple styles makes you a more effective and versatile coach.

Imagine that a pitcher in baseball throws the perfect curveball. He can strike out any right-handed player easily. However, this perfect curveball does not work well against someone who bats left-handed because the curve goes directly into their swing. Suddenly, the perfect pitch becomes useless, not because of the technique, but the situation itself. This holds true for your style as a coach, as well. No matter how excellent your methods are, if they don't mesh with a situation, they won't be effective.

If you are having a difficult time getting through to someone, don't automatically blame your coaching ability. It can be a matter of changing your approach.

Just like you don't need an actual certification for coaching, you do not need any licenses or certifications for the different coaching styles. Of course, the more training and experience you have, the better. The clients will also have more faith in you. Also, certain advanced techniques, like neuro-linguistic programming or hypnotherapy, require a certain level of knowledge to perform correctly. The general public is still skeptical about these certain techniques, and having some type of certification to back them up will give you more credibility. Look at it this way, how much trust would you have in someone who just walked up to you and said they know hypnotherapy?

We will now go over some coaching styles that you can incorporate into your coaching routine. Consider the advantages and disadvantages of each kind and how receptive different clients will be based on their personality. There is no one-size-fits-all approach, so it will behoove you to learn them all.

The Autocratic Style

Authoritarian

This is a highly structured coaching style where the control of the session lies squarely in the hands of the coach. The life coach acts like more of an authoritarian and develops a pre-established plan of action. With this method, the client is expected to follow the coach's lead without much room for deviation.

This type of style is used a lot for business coaching. The client will not receive a program tailor-made for them. The coach will be the authority figure, and the client must follow their directions.

This type of style works well for those who need discipline and structure. The client who needs immediate approaches to fix their circumstances will do well with an autocratic coach. As a coach, if you feel that your client needs to know exactly what is expected of them, use this practice to help them. If you give these individuals the freedom to come up with their own decisions, they will simply waver and fall into the abyss. Clients who respect authority will respect the autocratic coach.

To be an effective autocratic coach, you must encourage the following:

- Productivity
- Efficiency
- Trust in the coach
- Stress reduction
- Realistic goal attainment
- Reduced ambiguity

During urgent and pressing situations, the autocratic style reigns supreme above all else. This is because there is not much time for collaboration, and a single leader must take the helm. A person who wants to be told what to do, rather than guess, will appreciate listening to an authority figure.

The problem with this style is that a client can become overwhelmed and feel unheard. Even when a person wants you to take control, you still need to gauge the situation and allow them to make the final decision. Think of this as more of a structured approach to help the client come up with their own answers. That is what life coaching is all about.

Some people want to be in control of their lives and refuse to give up the reins to anyone else. This type of person will not benefit from an authoritarian style. If you are coaching someone with a strong personality who wants to make their own decisions, try a different method. There are plenty more to go over.

The Democratic Coaching Style

This type of style follows the same principles of a democracy. It takes into account the concerns, interests, and choices of the people involved. It is a much more inclusive and targeted approach than the strict autocratic style, and it allows room for more tailor-made programs. With this method, the client has a much bigger say in how the sessions go and in what way specific issues will be resolved. The client has as much control as the coach, or more.

The democratic style allows for a client to be introspective, have self-control, and be accountable for their decisions. Since they are the ones most in control, they assume much more accountability for the outcomes. Career coaching, financial coaching, and personal growth coaching are some examples where this style is most beneficial. These are the areas in life where a person needs more accountability.

This coaching style encourages the following:

- Motivation
- Teamwork and collaboration
- Self-efficacy
- Creativity
- Commitment to objectives
- Empowerment
- Productivity

If your client has a very hard time making decisions or has no clue what direction they should go, the democratic style might not be effective. The client will simply run around in circles without any real progress. The autocratic approach will be more appropriate in cases like these.

Holistic Coaching Style

You may have heard the term "holistic medicine," which views the whole person when providing medical treatment. It does not just focus on one area of the body or curing a single disease.

The holistic coaching style follows the same ideology in encompassing the whole person. The mindset of a holistic coach is that the body is one working unit and not a bunch of segmented parts. All areas must work in synchronicity with one another, or they will all cease to function at some point.

Therefore, a coach who follows this model must pay attention to their client's complete growth and encourage balance in all areas of their life. This is an ideal approach to use when you are getting to know a client because you will target all aspects of their being and really be able to figure out what their true strengths and weaknesses are.

The holistic style can provide a coaching client with perspective about their true place in the world. This will make them feel more connected, give them a sense of purpose, help them recognize why they matter, and understand how to get where they want to be.

Life coaches should strive to recognize their clients as a whole person. The holistic coaching style encourages the following benefits:

- Feeling understood
- Trust in the coach-client relationship
- Uncovering of feelings that are deeply held
- Enhanced well-being and functioning across the whole spectrum of a person and their life

This is a type of style that almost anyone will find appealing, especially when determining more in-depth issues that might be going on.

Laissez-Faire Coaching Style

This is the most hands-off coaching style, which works when a client has the ability to motivate themselves with minimal guidance from an outside source. In this approach, a life coach simply acts as a type of consultant who makes regular check-ups, but for the most part holds the client responsible as the primary owner of the process. Basically, the client comes up with their own methods of dealing with their issues, while the coach is available as a backup if needed.

The laissez-faire style has been criticized as being ineffective due to having zero leadership from the coach. Critics of this method point out the lack of leadership and responsibility as the coach shows virtually none of it during the process. However, proponents of this style feel it has a lot of value as long as there are regular performance follow-ups that are done. This style encourages the following:

- Self-empowerment
- Self-efficacy
- Self-management
- Freedom
- Decision-making abilities
- Autonomy

This style is probably not a good one to start off with and will work best with clients who have worked with a life coach for a while and are familiar with developing their own plans.

Transformational Coaching Style

This is a one-on-one approach that aims to build a trusting relationship between a coach and a client in which both parties agree upon the process and end goals. There is no hierarchy here as it is a 50-50 partnership. The coach will provide the authentic support and candid feedback when necessary.

This type of coaching style encourages the following:

- Collaborative skills
- Self-discovery
- Intrinsic motivation
- Accountability
- Problem-solving

Transactional Coaching

This is an exchanged-focused relationship between a coach and a client. It is aimed at promoting performance and getting rid of stumbling blocks. A few substyles of transactional coaching are rewards coaching, which is the offering of rewards for good performance; active management by exception, which is actively attending to the client's challenges; and passive management by exception, which is only intervening when problems become more advanced. Transactional coaching encourages:

- Problem-solving skills
- Performance enhancement
- Competency-building
- Goal clarity
- Short-term changes

Mindfulness Coaching

Mindfulness is the practice of becoming fully present in your situation. It means you are not thinking about the past or worrying about the future. You are simply at peace with the current moment. Mindfulness coaching draws from this philosophy by promoting a type of awareness in which a person starts paying attention to their present thoughts and feelings without any judgment.

The goal of this approach is to help a client respond to stress and anxiety in a calmer way. Mindfulness coaching encourages the following:

- Acceptance
- Peace of mind
- Clarity
- Reduced anxiety
- Awareness

- Harmony with the present moment.

There are more coaching styles that exist beyond the one mentioned here, but these are some of the most common ones practiced. Most clients you come across will benefit from one of these strategies, but as you move your coaching practice along, you may learn other methods for specific settings. Your personal coaching style will determine how you interact with your clients, so be aware of all of them and practice each one depending on what the situation calls for.

So far, we have gone over the life coaching process and various styles and techniques to make you the best in the field. Your clients will see you as an expert when you can change fluidly between various approaches and know when to use them accordingly. If you display uncertainty in your practices, your clients will be uncertain about you, which is not a good sign. There is still much more information to go over, so we are not done yet.

CHAPTER 5: GREAT QUESTIONS TO ASK WHEN COACHING SOMEONE

Questions?

As a life coach, you will be helping clients find many solutions in life. But instead of using the more orthodox manner of providing answers, you will instead be asking a lot more questions. These questions are meant to guide a conversation towards finding a solution, which the client will be able to come up with themselves. This will be a critical part of any coaching session, so you must know the right questions to ask, as well as how and when to ask them. The energy and demeanor you give off will set the tone for the interaction. Also, asking a brilliant question at the wrong time can be detrimental. You must gauge your client and determine what they are ready for.

The largest mistake life coaches make is trying to solve the problems for their clients. They are actually doing a disservice in this respect. People need to learn how to help themselves in order to get the best results in the long term. All of us have the answers to the challenges in our own life. We just need someone to point us in the right direction. Therefore, think of questions as directional points. If you guide someone into turning left when they should have gone right, they can end up on the wrong path. As you gain more experience, you will experience the power of asking the right questions.

You might have noticed that the first part of the word question is "quest," as in, you are on a 'quest' to find answers. This is why random questioning is not the way to go. There needs to be some sort of strategy involved.

MAKING A TRANSFORMATION

The magic of transformational coaching occurs when your client has foundational shifts in their neurology and thought process. Always remember that the work happens inside of your client's mind and not in your own mind. Use the following questions as a guide to help them uncover their personal solutions. We will break these down into separate sections.

Questions to Identify With Their Model of the World

Everyone has a different view of the world, and perception becomes reality. As a coach, it is important not to jump in with assumptions and automatically believe you understand someone and their issues. Also, never undercut what they are going through by making dismissive statements like, "You know, everyone has problems." While it's true, everyone has a unique set of circumstances that affect them differently.

Always create a positive rapport and a safe space for your clients. They should feel comfortable expressing their thoughts without the fear of judgment. With these questions, you are attempting to learn their model of the world, and not necessarily change it. For this to occur, you must come from a place of curiosity without actually jumping into their thoughts. The following are some great questions to help you identify with your client.

- What is the problem from your perspective?
- What is this particular problem making you say about yourself?
- What have you tried before in a similar situation that has worked, if anything?
- Similarly, what have you tried in a similar situation that has not worked?

- What are you telling yourself about the possible solutions?
- What are you really afraid of here? (Everyone has unique fears that may be vastly different than your own.)
- What beliefs do you have about yourself, in general?
- What beliefs do you have about the world, in general?
- What do you really want out of your life?
- What is really important to you?
- What habits do you currently possess that support your goals?
- What habits do you have that may sabotage your goals?

After asking these in-depth questions, you will have a great idea of how your client identifies with the world. You may learn things that surprise you and that you never even thought of. Remember, though, the questions are not about you, so just listen to the answers without any preconceived notions.

Questions for Getting Leverage and Permission

This relates to how ready the client is to make changes and how well you can convince them to do so. Before you enter this phase of questions, you must ensure your client is on board to move forward. If not, keep digging until you get to the necessary readiness for change. Once your client is at that point, proceed with these questions to get leverage:

- If you don't make this change, what will it mean to you?
- If you don't make this change, what will it cost you? (This is not about finances, but anything valuable in their lives.)
- What's missing in your life?
- Who in your life is missing out?
- Who else does your current pattern of behavior possibly hurt?
- When will you know that you have suffered enough?
- How will you know that you are ready to change now?

The remainder of the questions are geared for getting permission:

- Do you want to clear this up now? As in, are you ready to start taking action today, at this moment?
- Would you like help with this issue right now?
- Would you give me full permission to be your life coach and help you through this?
- Are you ready to access your unconscious mind to eliminate this problem and have conscious awareness of the change?

After these sets of questions, you will have full leverage and permission to help the person. Of course, that is if they agree to it.

Questions for Determining New Outcomes

Have your client clearly define their new desired outcomes. What do they want to be feeling, thinking, and experiencing, etc. when the coaching session is completed? Have them be crystal clear about their outcomes, and don't let them get away with being generalized. Make sure they are coming up with this on their own and you are not urging them in any direction. Even if you think a certain route will be better for them, only the client can decide this ultimately. The following are some great questions to ask for determining new outcomes:

- What are you not experiencing right now that you want to experience?
- What are you experiencing right now that you no longer want to experience?
- What would you like to happen for you?
- How do you want to feel?
- What would all of this look like?
- Paint me a picture of everything in your mind, and be as descriptive as possible. Who is there with you? What do you see all around you? What do you hear and smell? What can you touch? What are you thinking and not thinking? What emotions are you feeling on the inside?

OPEN-ENDED QUESTIONS

You may have noticed that most of these questions are open-ended rather than definitive, or closed. Closed-ended questions will result in abrupt answers with little to no opportunity for advancement. Open-ended questions allow you to seek out more answers with your client, which are more likely to lead to proper solutions. Avoid closed-ended questions like:

- Are you happy today?
- Are you feeling good this morning?
- Did you sleep well last night?
- Is there anything you want to go over?

Most of these types of questions can be answered with a simple 'yes' or 'no.' You might be able to question a little further, in some cases. However, it is best to stick with open-ended questions.

(Cesario, n.d.)

MORE TIPS FOR ASKING THE APPROPRIATE QUESTIONS

We have given you a few suggestions already for asking the appropriate questions, at the appropriate times, and in the appropriate ways. Basically, the questions need to be appropriate. After asking specific questions, you need to listen intently to what your client says and then ask good follow-up questions as needed. In this section, we will go over some crucial tips to help you understand how to ask the best questions in your coaching practice.

- Make your questions exploratory and experimental. Do not be harsh or direct with your questions, or your client can feel rushed and thrown off.

- Help your client when they need help in articulating their feelings. You are not telling them what their feelings are, but just clarifying them so you both understand.

- A question to ask in this instant could be: If that feeling you're describing could speak, what would it say?

- Help your client imagine their own success, and then plan from their perspective. The theory here is that it's easier to come up with solutions if a person imagines already being in the reality of the goal.

- Occasionally pause to help your client look more deeply within themselves. The question "what do you need to see here?" is used to help your client gain more insight into a current situation.

- Obtain evidence about what someone means. For instance, if they say that they want to be happy, what does that mean to them? What is their vision of happiness?

- Get your clients to keep themselves on track. It's not just about establishing goals, but implementing them too. As a coach, you don't tell your clients how to stay on track; they must decide that on their own.

- Find out what motivates your client. Literally ask them: What motivates you? This is a great way to get to know your clients and what inspires them to keep moving forward.

- Help your clients help themselves. Do not carry the burden of their problems. Provide a safe space for them and ask in-depth, non-judgemental questions that will help them find solutions on their own.

- A good question to ask here is: How can you best support yourself right now?

- Find out what in a client's life cannot be taken away from them even if the worst happened. This does not have to be a material possession. It is usually something about their core values.

- Find a way for your clients to give themselves good advice. The client will know themselves best, so they will provide the best advice that will help their situation.

- Have your client imagine their ideal situation in the future and then ask them what advice their future self would give their present self.

- Determine what positive intention exists behind a destructive decision. Most individuals do things because they achieve some type of benefits from it. Even if it's something minor, it is enough to motivate them to keep moving.

- Determine your client's 'why.' Why do they want to do the things they do? What is whispering inside of them that is aching to come out? Don't just assume a client will know the answers to these questions, and don't think that your 'why' is the same as theirs.

- Search for your client's deepest truths. Ask them directly what their truth is, and give them plenty of time to search for it.

As you practice your life coaching techniques, you will become much more familiar with how to ask the right questions. We advise that you practice on family and close friends before trying it on strangers. You can even practice by asking yourself some good questions. Just remember the core principles about asking the proper questions. Never make your client feel like they are rushed, and don't answer the questions for them. They need to come up with their own answers.

SOME MORE QUESTIONS

Like we said, asking questions is one of the most important aspects of life coaching. You will not have the answers for your clients. They will have the answers, and you just have to help find them. We will finish off this chapter by going over some of the best questions a life coach can ask during a session (Elsey, 2019).

- What would you like to have achieved by the end of this session? This is a great question to ask at the beginning of a coaching session so the client and coach are perfectly clear on what they're working on. This will bring great value to the session because it keeps everyone on track from the get-go.

- Out of everything you might have, what is one thing that is missing in your life right now? This question will help your client with determining unmet needs. You can also ask your client what they want more or less of in their lives.

- If there is anything you can change right now, what would it be? This is a great question to ask when a client is feeling overwhelmed and cannot get focused. This will help them remain grounded.

- How will you know when your desired goal has been achieved? Many people are not clear about their goals, so they never take action towards them. A question like this helps your client get more specific, so they know how to proceed.

- What is an initial step you can take right now? This question is great for larger goals. It will help a client get started. From here, you two can come up with further action steps that will move the client forward little by little. In this question, you can include steps to take over the next week, month, year, etc.

- What do you not want me to ask you? You can ask this question in a playful way, but it is really to get to know what areas of their life they are avoiding. You can stay away from these areas at first and revisit them when the time is right.

- How does what you are doing serve you? This question can be directed at behavior that is self-sabotaging. This will help them take stock of how their current behavior patterns are either benefiting or hurting them. You can also ask the client what the benefit is of staying right where they are.

- How will you celebrate your victories? Celebrations are often overlooked, but they are a necessity during the growth process. Encouraging your clients to celebrate accomplishments will allow them to pause and take everything in. Otherwise, life will become a repetition of forgetful moments. In other words, stop and smell the roses once in a while.

- What areas of your life are not going well right now, and which ones are absolutely awesome? This is a great question to ask when your client is overly focused on making a great future but cannot focus on what's great now.

- What was the biggest win for you during the session today? Obviously, this question comes at the end and will help the client think about the benefits of coaching. As a coach, you will also understand what your clients get the most out of during a regular session.

Using the questions we went over in this chapter as an example, and come up with some of your own questions too. As you become more familiar with the process, you will be able to ask some very helpful questions that can be life-changing for your clients. Remember, even though these questions seem simple, many individuals never think about them deeply because they get so caught up in the craziness of life. You can assist them in becoming more grounded.

7

THE SCIENCE OF HABITS

How many times have you made a New Year's resolution, or heard somebody make one themselves, only to not follow through on it in any way? Or, they stuck to their new goals for a few days and then went back to their old ways? Some common resolutions people will make are to start eating healthy and going to the gym regularly. Unfortunately, they do not stick to these new goals. A common joke that's out there is to open a gym called 'Resolutions,' which turns into a bar after the first two weeks of January.

The point is, resolutions often fail because people are just motivating themselves through an arbitrary date on the calendar, but doing nothing to enforce new behavior in their lives. In order to follow through on these resolutions, these individuals must actively change their habits. Our habits are built up over time by practices we follow on a regular basis. To change these, we must alter our thought process and therefore adjust our behavior. Only then will we be able to follow through on our goals, whatever they may be.

HABITS AND THEIR FORMATION

A habit is defined as a regular tendency or practice that an individual has which is often hard to give up. People tend to develop strange tendencies as they grow older, which can be rooted in ideas that they learned as a child. For example, if a child's parents made them wake up every morning at five, that child will likely keep that routine until adulthood. It is what they are used to, and they have adapted both physically and mentally to this practice.

Habits can define us in many ways and also determine our future. There is a reason why some people perpetually succeed in life, while others always fall short. Some people lead healthy lives, while others suffer from chronic health issues. Some individuals always win, while others cannot catch a break. Yes, luck does play a role. However, if a person is always being dealt a bad hand, then continuously blaming it on misfortunes is just playing the victim card.

We are not denying that some people have it harder than others; however, everyone can still adjust their behaviors to improve their lives. The biggest problem that arises from bad lack is not poverty, poor health, or a lack of resources. Instead, it is the adaptation of bad habits, which are extremely hard to break.

Why Are Habits Difficult to Change?

According to Newton's Law of Motion, every object that is in a uniform state of motion tends to remain in that same state until some type of external force is applied to it. Of course, this external force does not have to be visible. For example, in the case of throwing an object into the air, gravity will only let it get so far before turning its trajectory back downwards. To summarize, objects in motion tend to stay in motion until something comes along to stop them.

The concept of the Law of Motion can also be attributed to human behavior, especially in regard to changing habits. Once a habit is developed, momentum takes over and the behavior keeps on going. The longer a person has had the habit, the more momentum it will have. The habits we develop go all the way down to our core and infiltrate every aspect of our being. This means we get a certain emotional and physiological response when we perform certain behaviors, and they make us feel good. Making that first shift is always the hardest part.

The difficulty in habit adjustment goes way beyond willpower. Our subconscious and unconscious minds, which are not immediately accessible in everyday life, are where habits form for the long term. This area of the mind is controlled by the basal ganglia in our brains. When we perform an action multiple times, it starts to get embedded in our brains. The actions we have been performing for years are so deeply embedded that they become a part of us, like an appendage. Therefore, it takes much less effort to repeat these activities than it does to engage in new ones.

Basically, to change a habit, we must force ourselves to do things on the conscious level, where we have immediate control, until our basal ganglia take over. At this point, our subconscious mind gets involved and a new habit starts forming. It really is a simple formula, but not easy in practice.

Think about habits as your brain's version of autopilot. Basically, you are performing tasks without even thinking about them. For routine activities, like getting ready for work or making breakfast, they can be a blessing. On the other hand, when we become comfortable, we start to develop bad habits without even realizing it. For example, instead of getting out of bed right away when the alarm goes off, we push the snooze button multiple times. Instead of making a healthy breakfast, we settle for a Pop-Tart and a sugar-filled coffee. Instead of going to bed at a reasonable time, we end up watching YouTube videos until midnight. Oh yeah, and don't forget about that late-night snack.

Bad habits are easier to slip into than good ones because they generally require less resistance. For instance, it is easier to sleep an extra hour every morning than it is to get up and exercise. It is easier to eat junk food because it often provides an immediate rush, rather than health food, which usually provides its benefits over the long run. The thirst for quick gratification is why negative habits are easier to form.

Let's Talk About Formation

Anybody that has tried to set a goal knows exactly how difficult it can be. Except for a few rare exceptions, changes do not occur overnight. It takes continuous effort and there will be many peaks and valleys along the way. Meaning, success never goes in a straight, upward trajectory.

When you are trying to make positive changes in your life, getting up and motivating yourself can become exhausting and drain all of your energy. If a person had to do this every day, being able to sustain it for the long run would be near impossible. This is where habit formation comes to our aid. While motivating yourself to make changes will be difficult for a while, as our new routines become ingrained into our subconscious minds, we will start performing them naturally.

For example, if you always hit the snooze alarm and wake up 30 minutes later than you plan, but want to change this, it will take time to get used to. On the first day, try waking up 10 minutes earlier than you used to. The next morning, go for 20 minutes. Finally, on the third day, wake up 30 minutes earlier than you're used to. From here, keep motivating yourself to wake up at this time. Day after day, it will become easier because your body and mind will become used to it. Eventually, waking up at the desired time will become natural, and you might not even need an alarm clock. Once you reach this state of habit formation, you are using much less energy to keep everything going.

Many experts believe that a habit takes about 21 days to form if focused on continuously. This is just an average and should not be taken as absolute gospel. However, you need to realize that a habit does take a while to form, so do not give up. If it's taking you longer than the average time, don't take it so hard. Everyone develops at their own pace, and it's important to remain consistent.

Let's go over some nuggets of wisdom related to habits. These will give you a better idea of how habits affect our lives, so they are easier to understand and manage.

Habits Emerge Without Our Consent

According to Charles Duhigg of *The Power of Habits* (The Coaching Academy Blog, n.d.) fame, the brain uses habits to help save energy to make important decisions. The brain will often implement what worked before in a certain situation, without our consent. In order to change this, we have to actively oppose it. As an example, if we come home from work every day and grab a soda from the fridge, our brain will know this every time and cause the same action to occur. If we are to change this activity, we must force ourselves to do something different. One day, we can reach for a healthy drink, like fresh juice or plain water. If we do this again for the next several days, our brain will start recognizing this pattern and start taking this step without our consent, until we decide to make another change.

Habit formation Has a Clear Pattern

The simple pattern for habit formation is a trigger, followed by a routine, followed by a reward. For instance, hunger can be the trigger, eating a snack can be the routine, and the feeling of being satiated can be the reward. The focal point here is the routine. What are you doing to satisfy the trigger, and what type of reward are you getting from the routine?

Think Small

This may sound confusing, but when it comes to habits, think small. When you are building a new habit, do not try to change everything at once. Instead, focus on small, repetitive steps that ultimately lead to big changes. If your plan is to begin an exercise routine, do not go to the gym on the first day and go crazy for an hour with the most insane workouts. All you have to do is feed your trigger, and it does not matter how long. So, on the first day, work out for five to 10 minutes, and increase the time from there. Put on those gym clothes every day and get to work. Whether you do 10 minutes or 30 minutes, you are creating a habit slowly.

Hone in on Your Triggers

This pattern provides a strong framework for building new habits with manageable steps. It allows you to focus on what is important to you and not become overwhelmed by major goals. Also, when you know that your bad habits start with a certain trigger, you can work on breaking these habits.

As an example, a heavy drinker may get into the habit of drinking several cans of beer at night while watching TV. In this case, watching TV is the trigger because it incites the person into having a few drinks. Once the individual realizes this, they can focus on changing their drinking habit by either replacing it with a new one or getting rid of the trigger.

Begin With the End in Mind

Before you break your goal down into smaller steps, visualize and understand what you want your end result to be. Think about your goal, and then break it down into manageable steps. Also, determine what smaller habits you need to develop to reach your objective. Will you need to learn a new skill, get some more training, or shift your mindset in some way? Take all of these into consideration and be as detailed as you can.

You Must Believe You Can Change

It can be easy to switch from a bad habit to a good one for a short-term period. However, to stick with it, you must have a belief in yourself that you can. If you don't believe in yourself, your new habits will fall apart quickly and you will relapse into your old routine.

It All Starts With a Good Start

There have been many schools of thought pointing to the fact that a good morning routine sets you up for a successful day ahead. There is plenty of anecdotal evidence to support this, as some of the most successful individuals in their field have a set morning ritual they adhere to. They wake up at a certain time, work out, eat a healthy breakfast, read, and plan for the day ahead. When they get their day started right, it sets a positive tone for the next several hours.

People like Jocko Willink, Tim Ferris, Oprah Winfrey, Barack Obama, and Tony Robbins work hard to win their mornings. Their devout morning routines help them gain focus, clarity, and energy to attack the day. For example, Tony Robbins does deep breathing exercises, followed by a cold shower. Oprah Winfrey performs meditation, followed by running on the treadmill to get her heart pumping (Adams, 2017).

What do you do every morning? If your routine is not inspiring and getting you ready to attack the day, you need to change quickly. Some examples of positive morning rituals include:

- Waking up early
- Exercising
- Reading
- Planning the day ahead
- Mindfulness practices
- Spending time with family

Author Amy Landino (The Coaching Academy Blog, n.d.) breaks down in her book *Good Morning, Good Life* how to successfully build habits for the morning that will set you up for a successful day. The key idea here is that the morning routine is not the actual goal, but the path towards the goal. It really doesn't matter what you do, as long as you can take time before the responsibilities of the day to reflect on yourself and your goals, and to take control of the day ahead. If you don't take time to focus on yourself, the day will rule you.

Choose the Habits You Want to Keep

Our daily routines often become cluttered with habits we don't especially enjoy or get anything out of. We just happened to develop them over time based on our experiences. This can lead to goals that we want nothing to do with. When we start focusing on habits that spark our joy, we can find more clarity on what type of life we actually want to live.

∾

Habits Lead to Freedom

Many people believe that habits are too constraining. As a result, they become resistant to them. However, much of the literature provides a different perspective. Developing certain habits can provide you with more time, freedom, and energy for the things that are truly important to you.

For example, paying bills is never fun, but getting into the habit of paying them at a certain time every month can reduce stress and worry because it becomes natural. Eventually, you will sit down to pay your bills without even thinking about it. This will allow you to focus more on things you actually enjoy.

WHEN YOU'RE FINALLY READY TO MAKE A CHANGE

I don't want you to become disillusioned here. Changing habits can be difficult, but it is not impossible. If you follow specific strategies, you can begin altering your thought patterns, and eventually, your behavior. As a result, you will create significantly different outcomes. After changing your habits from negative to positive, you will finally start realizing why some people win and others lose. It is not limited to talent, skill, or genetic factors. The actions you commit to on a daily basis are what have the largest impact on your life. Therefore, the routine you develop is what determines the end goal.

The right time to start changing habits is when you decide to do so. Do not wait for an arbitrary date, like January 1st or another special occasion. When you are ready to make some changes, it's the right time to begin. If you want to start waking up early, do it tomorrow. Don't tell yourself you'll start after a week or after a certain moment in your life passes. These are just excuses, and you need to start nipping them in the bud.

As you go through changes, there will be many ups and downs, and plenty of mistakes will be made. This is okay because your goal is to take action and not to be perfect. Nobody is perfect, and trying to be is just a waste of time. Perfectionism makes you less productive because you are focused too heavily on something that is unattainable. Changing habits requires consistency, and some days you will be able to do more than others. As long as you are performing, you are progressing. If you exercise for 45 minutes one day and 30 minutes the next, don't be hard on yourself. At least you exercised consistently, which is the goal.

Finally, you must learn to embrace the power of triggers. They are what motivate you to perform a certain habit, whether good or bad. Focus on triggers that remind you to perform good habits, and ditch the ones that cause you to perform bad habits. If you are a regular smoker and love to light up when you're watching TV or hanging out at a bar, then you need to either modify these triggers or get rid of them completely. For example, while watching TV, you can sit in a different area of the room and you may not get the same cravings. If this doesn't work, figure out other ways to make changes.

Focus on triggers that result in positive attitudes. If you routinely go into the kitchen to grab a snack from a bowl, start filling that bowl with healthy fruits instead of candy. When you wake up in the morning, keep your phone away from you so you are not tempted to scroll through the first thing in the morning. Place a book on your nightstand so it is the first item you grab in the morning.

I will now go over some specific action steps to help change your bad habits. These strategies can work with whatever bad habit you are trying to change or replace. My advice to you is to focus on one habit at a time and prioritize with the most critical one. For example, if you have negative habits that are putting your health at risk, you may want to start with those and work your way down. Perhaps your money managing skills are poor and they are causing you to go into bankruptcy. Determine what areas in your life are harming you the most and go from there.

Acknowledge

Before you can fix a problem, you must recognize that it exists. Therefore, you must acknowledge a bad habit before you can start working on it. If you are in denial, you will get nowhere. I don't want you to think of yourself as weak. Bad habits exist for everyone, and it takes a lot of courage to admit to them. Once you wrap your head around your issues, it will become easier to manage them. It's similar to going into the hospital time and time again and not knowing why, but then finally getting a diagnosis. Even if it's kind of grim, actually knowing what you're dealing with will give you a fighting chance.

Acknowledging your bad habit is just like recognizing who your enemy is, and you will make a huge breakthrough by doing this. Give yourself credit for making it this far, because many people do not. Unfortunately, they live with the mindset that having any flaws is a bad thing, so they always deny doing anything wrong. This is just the first step, so let's keep going.

Understand

After acknowledging a bad habit, you must understand why you want or need to break it. This will become your ultimate reason. Is the bad habit causing you poor health, ruining your relationships, and negatively impacting your career? For example, you might be staying up late watching YouTube videos or eating a heavy meal right before going to bed, both of which are affecting your sleep patterns. Determine your reason for wanting to break free of your bad habits.

Habits are not limited to our actions, but also include our thoughts. If you constantly think negatively about any situation, that is a negative habit. Your emotional state can also be a trigger for other poor choices. For instance, when you're sad, you might overeat or drink excessively. When you are angry, you might start getting violent and breaking things. Focus on these cues and the relationship they have to your bad habits.

To fully understand your bad habits, you must step out of your comfort zone and have a full look at yourself from an outside perspective. Imagine sitting on a rooftop and watching yourself live your life. After acknowledging your bad habits and understanding why they exist, it will be easier to picture a different life for yourself. Okay, the first two steps of habit change are down. Now, we move onto the third step.

Shift

"The speed of new habit pattern development is largely determined by the intensity of the emotion that accompanies the decision to begin acting in a particular way."

— BRIAN TRACY

Our emotions that we carry with each habit will play a huge role in how quickly and intensely we reject bad habits and focus on the good ones. Both actions can be equally difficult. Since habits include both thoughts and actions, it is imperative to shift the way we think about and deal with our routines. If you want to start waking up early, not only do you have to perform the action of getting out of bed at a certain time, you must also have a positive way of thinking about it. If your thoughts revert to how tired you are and how miserable it will feel to leave your comfy bed, then it's a long shot that you will continue this habit for the long haul.

In addition to getting out of bed, you have to think about the benefits that come with it. For instance, getting out of bed earlier will allow you to get a good workout in, which will release endorphins to make you feel better. Also, getting out of bed early will give you more time to plan your day, eat a nutritious breakfast, and perform various other self-care activities. When you are shifting your habits, do it with your thoughts as well as your actions, and your chances of success will increase immensely.

When you transition the way you think, you are already programming your mind to know what it feels like to practice your new routines. In the case of working out in the morning, thinking about the endorphin release that will come out will allow your mind to already know what will happen post-exercise. When your mind and body are working in synchronicity, it is an amazing combination. Practice thinking only about positive outcomes to the point you will have no room to think about anything negative. Imagine your mind as a compartment with limited space. Why fill it with things that you don't want in there, like your negative thoughts? Clear those out, put new ones in, and never allow empty space for old thoughts to return. You will transition from bad habits to good habits in no time.

Visualize

It is now time to visualize a life filled with new, positive habits. Once you shift your focus to the benefits of forming new routines and rituals, it will be easy to picture your new life. This life will be filled with your positive habits and the abundance that comes with performing them. If your goal was to get up earlier every morning, visualize what your life will look like in the near future because of this action. Will you be in better shape because you exercised more and ate healthy meals? Will your career take off because you made more time to plan your day ahead? Finally, will your personal and familial relationships improve because you dedicated more time to them?

When you visualize, be very detailed in what you want to see. What time are you waking up and going to bed? Where are you working? What city, or even country, are you living in? How much energy are you feeling throughout the day? What emotions are running through your mind?

Practicing visualization allows you to get a head start on living your dream life. You need to visualize on a consistent basis. You can even make it part of your morning and nightly ritual. Doing it when you first wake up in the morning can motivate you into having a more productive day. You will realize that you are working towards this ideal life you have imagined. Not only will training your mind to see what your new habits will bring you to make it easier to stick with them, but your mind will also think you are already there.

Reward

Okay, you are done now, so let's party! No, I am just kidding. In all seriousness, though, habit formation is not easy. It will take a lot of time, effort, and discipline on your part. You should be proud of the milestones you accomplish, so take the time to reward yourself along the way. Do not go overboard and fall off the wagon, but definitely perform acts that are rewarding to you. For example, if you have started a healthier meal plan and have been executing it for several weeks, then give yourself a cheat meal, or even cheat day. Just don't allow it to turn into several cheat days or weeks. Also, give yourself a pat on the back regularly. Sit down in a quiet space and think about what you have already accomplished.

Embrace your new changes that developed from healthier habits. Use these changes to inspire you to keep moving forward. Think about life as a constant learning and growing experience. You will never become perfect, so there are always areas you can improve upon. Out with the old and in with the new, as the old adage states.

WHAT'S IN A DAY? OR 21?

Every one of us grows at a different pace. Depending on the individuals, it can take anywhere from a few days to several weeks, or even months, to officially form a new habit. However, many experts believe that 21 days is the average amount of time it takes. The number was first referenced by Dr. Maxwell Maltz (Clear, 2018) who was an American cosmetic surgeon, and author of the book *Psycho-Cybernetics*. He noticed in his patients that it took about 21 days for them to come to terms with their new image after an extensive procedure. This was more of a situational observation by Dr. Maltz, and not really an in-depth study.

As his book became more popular, so did the 21-day theory. Several experts began tying it to habit formation, and it began getting known as factual. All we can say is that you can use this 21-day model as a guide, but don't take it as gospel. What you can do is expect to follow a certain routine for a minimum of 21 days, or three weeks, before it becomes natural to you. Once again, don't just assume this will be the case. Don't be discouraged if you are at the 21-day mark and don't feel like your new habit has formed. In addition, do not just slack off after the three-week period. Your new habit should be a lifelong transformation and not just a quick fix.

HOW A LIFE COACH CAN HELP WITH HABIT CHANGE

If you decide to pursue a career in life coaching, a large portion of your time will be spent helping your clients with habit changes. As their coach, you can be there as a guide and they will have to come to their own realizations. You can also be the outside perspective they need. People often cannot see the forest through the trees, which means they are way too closed off within themselves to see what issues they have going on.

During the first step of habit change, the coach can assist their client in recognizing the negative areas of their life and what might be causing them. From here, they can come in contact with their bad habits. After this, they can acknowledge their existence. The coach can help ease their anxiety by letting them know it takes strength to admit faults.

After helping your client acknowledge their poor habits, assist them in understanding what negative effects they are causing. The client will start seeing how much of an impact their routines have on their outcomes, and this can inspire them to make some changes. Once again, let your client know they are doing the right thing and are not weak for recognizing areas where they need improvement.

Now, you can help your client come up with strategies to make adjustments. Give them the tools to start thinking about the positive aspects of new habit formations. Also, help them start visualizing. You can use a few minutes during your session to help them come up with a picture-perfect life. You will notice a major change in their mindset and actions.

Of course, you need to hold your client accountable too because it is ultimately up to them. They need to do the work; you are just there to provide support. When you see progress, provide encouragement and congratulate them on their accomplishments. Provide some instructions on how they can reward themselves for reaching personal milestones.

As a life coach, you can help your client improve their career, social life, health, relationships, and so much more by guiding them in changing their habits. Not everyone can do it on their own. However, everyone has the power to do so, but just needs a little direction. This is where true life coaching comes into play.

Never discount the power of rituals. Think of each habit you possess as a building block of a large structure. If one of the building blocks is dysfunctional, the structure might lean. If there are enough dysfunctional building blocks, then the structure might fall over altogether. Your goal should be to eliminate as many negative building blocks in the structure or your life so that you do not fall apart. Good luck on your habit formation journey!

PROMOTING A HABIT CHALLENGE

A great way to help your client develop a new habit and hold them accountable at the same time is to promote a habit challenge. This is where you challenge them to come up with a habit they want to change or form, and then give them a certain time limit to follow through on it. Now, this deadline is not meant for the full development of the new habit. As we said, everyone works on their own timeline. However, this can push them to stay on track with their goals and make serious improvements in their lives.

To begin, pick an arbitrary number like 21, 25, or 30. This is the number of days your client is required to follow through on their chosen ritual. For example, if it is to exercise for at least 15 minutes every morning, the challenge is to do this for the set number of days straight. So, if the decided number is 30, your client will have to exercise 15 minutes every day for 30 days straight, rain or shine.

After the 30 days, assess your client and ask how easy they find their new routine. If they feel like it's natural and they can do it easily, you can use this same challenge for other habits. See for yourself how this method works.

8

THE MINDSET COACHING

Think about your mind as a set of pathways that are built over time. The building blocks are our thoughts and actions. When we repeat these thoughts and actions continuously, they further cement the pathways for us. After a while, these avenues in our minds are completely set. Therefore, it becomes effortless to think and do the same things over and over again. We create a natural pattern that flows like an electrical current through wires. In order to change these wires, we have to actively restructure them. We literally must take them down and rebuild them in a different order. After this, our thoughts and actions will be vastly different.

For instance, people tend to believe negative thoughts because it takes less of a struggle than thinking positively. As a result, they become natural for us, and our minds automatically revert to this way of thinking without allowing a positive thought to enter. This becomes our mindset, and we are stuck with it until we decide to do something about it. This is where a certain type of life coaching comes into play: the mindset coach.

A mindset coach can help to rewire an individual's mindset so they can start realizing their full potential. After working with a mindset coach, people end up becoming the best versions of themselves. Mainly, they start believing in themselves. Like any other type of life coach, they avoid giving direct advice, and rather guide their clients in finding their own answers.

Right now, you might be wondering how all of this occurs. The process is actually simple, but it will take effort on everyone's part. It involves preparing an individual to develop a thought process that is solid and geared towards a better life. This new thought process will help them embrace changes and make difficulties in their life appear like a cakewalk.

After working with a mindset coach, a client will feel a significant boost in their energy. People underestimate just how much their way of thinking affects their energy levels and productivity. However, negative thinking drains our energy and can mentally paralyze us into accomplishing nothing. A mindset coach will help develop more willpower in their clients, and therefore make them more optimistic about their circumstances.

The real change that occurs happens from within a client, where the best answers come from. This is why a mindset coach will heavily promote self-efficacy. As such, the coach must let their clients know they are capable of doing extraordinary things. Remember that people who succeed at the highest level were once ordinary people who did extraordinary things.

Throughout history, many people have risen from the ashes in some of the worst conditions anyone can know and created an abundance for themselves that most people cannot even imagine. They had it within them to make significant changes, not because they have superpowers, but a super will. If they can do it, so can you. One of the things you have to start doing is something we have promoted excessively in this book, and that's imagining. Use your imagination, just like when you were a kid.

YOU ARE HERE TO DO EXTRAORDINARY THINGS

Yes, a mindset coach can help their clients in many aspects of their lives. They guide people in so many ways. For example, the client might be going through a major career change. This could be changing job titles, changing companies, coming back to work after getting laid off, or even starting a business. The mindset coach can assist them in taking the first step, which is often the most crucial one. Once a client gets started, the mindset coach can continue to provide guidance and encouragement through all of the difficult moments. Sometimes, having a cheerleader in your corner is essential—someone who will believe in you enough to hold you accountable.

A mindset coach can also help people with changes in their lifestyle. A person might be transitioning to new surroundings, whether it's a new house, town, or even a new country altogether. This can also relate to new work environments that come with a career change. Change is very scary and uncomfortable, no matter who you are. Even if the change is necessary, a lot of uncertainty can come with it. Uncertainty can become crippling for people, especially if they are not used to it. A mindset coach can help provide some clarity during moments of mass confusion. They will guide an individual on how to enjoy and embrace their new lifestyle. They can even help clients realize their new situation is better than their old one. After this, it's out with the old and in with the new.

Sometimes, people feel stuck and don't know where to go. There can be many reasons for this or no reason at all. They are just in a position they don't want to be in and can't figure out how to get out of it. All of us fall into a rut, and it can be very frustrating and even depressing. It's like falling into a shallow pit, where you can see the light, but have no idea how to climb out. A mindset coach can help with the transition process in this type of scenario. They can revive someone's energy and help them to thrive by providing encouragement and an outside perspective. Sometimes, people just need a little nudge, and the mindset coach can give it to them.

A mindset coach can help clear all of the noise that exists in the world. Sometimes, the answers are there, but it's too loud to hear them. You need to block out that noise to stay focused. After working with a mindset coach, people will start to realize their true purpose in the world. Despite all of the craziness, every individual plays a valuable role in the world, and we must never forget that.

"None can destroy iron, but its own rust can! Likewise, none can destroy a person, but its own mindset can."

— RATAN TATA

Iron is one of the most durable materials on the planet. It is powerful enough to build train tracks and versatile enough to make amazing products. A train track made of iron can have countless trains running across it for years and years and still hold its original strength. You can burn it, freeze it, or throw it into the ocean, and it will still remain iron. However, when the rust builds up long enough, the piece of iron begins to rot and will eventually destroy itself. To prevent this from happening, the rust needs to be cleared on a regular basis.

The same concept applies to our mindset. Think of your mindset as a piece of iron. Now, picture everything in your surroundings, like insults, criticisms, failures, and losses, as the rust that is trying to destroy you, as all of the environmental factors try to destroy the iron. They won't destroy you, but they can alter your mindset towards the negative, which will ultimately bring you down if you don't clear all of it out. Once again, this is where the skills of a mindset coach come into play. They will help remove the metaphorical rust from your life.

WHO CAN USE A MINDSET COACH?

The short answer is everyone. A mindset coach can help a person in many different situations in life, including career, health, and relationships. Our mindset impacts every area of our lives and if we want to be successful, we must have the right thought processes. If you don't believe you can accomplish something, then you won't. It's as simple as that.

Now, will failures still occur? They definitely will. However, the great thing about having a positive mindset is that it gives you the strength, endurance, and clarity to keep charging through the low points in your life. With a negative mindset, a person sees no hope and simply gives up. Furthermore, a mindset coach will help lift a person up when they do fall down and make sure they keep that positive mindset.

After hearing about all the ways a mindset coach can help someone, are you ready to go down this path? We hope so, because it is a great avenue to make real changes in a person's life. You can also make a great living for yourself, as long as you know who to sell your services to. A large part of the coaching business is marketing since this is how you will ultimately obtain your clients. Even if you are the best coach in the world, if nobody knows about you, then you will ultimately get nowhere.

Now, let's return to the original question of this section: Who needs a mindset coach? Rather than bore you with too many details, we will provide some anecdotes to help clarify where and when a mindset coach can come in.

- Mike is a senior vice president of a major corporation. While he has had much career success in the past, he is currently going through a crisis. It is weighing down on him heavily and he cannot perform well. As more time passes, he is becoming less motivated.
- Mike can definitely use a mindset coach in this example. The coach will help him understand what is creating issues in his life and help find ways to move forward.
- Jenny has achieved high levels of success in her career. The sky's the limit for her, but she needs some extra motivation to reach her next promotion.
- A mindset coach can help Jenny dig deep down to find her motivation and give her the extra boost she needs.
- Benny is a new entrepreneur with a great idea. However, he does not know how to proceed forward with his venture, plus he needs a lot of self-improvement in his personal life.
- A mindset coach can determine what areas Benny

needs the most help in and then assist him in taking the first steps towards building his enterprise.

- Kenneth is a very successful salesperson. In fact, he could literally be the poster child for sales. Recently, his sales have been going down and he cannot figure out why. He is getting depressed and anxious and no longer knows what to do.

- A mindset coach can help Kenneth determine what changes have been made and why his sales have been going down. From here, they can both figure out if it's something Kenneth can control, and how.

These are just a few examples, and we can come up with many more. Think about some situations in your own life where you could have used a mindset coach. We are sure that you can find plenty. Also, think about people who have been through many struggles and just needed someone to guide them. All of these individuals, and others like them, are your potential customers.

HOW DOES A MINDSET COACH HELP?

We will now get into some specific strategies that a mindset coach can use to help. Also, remember that the skills and techniques discussed in the earlier chapters can apply here too. When you become aware of the many benefits of mindset coaching, you can educate your potential clients about them too.

So, let's go over some ways a mindset catch can help those who need them.

Building Self-Awareness

People will turn to their family and friends to learn more about themselves. They will ask them what they think and how they should behave. Furthermore, they will let people tell them what to do with their lives. Taking this a step further, people will rely on the opinions of neighbors, coworkers, acquaintances, and even total strangers to learn about who they are. The major problem here is that these individuals will come from an area of complete bias. They will not come from an objective viewpoint. Even if they don't have a bias, they will make other blunders like giving out lectures or directly telling people what to do.

In order to gain self-awareness, people must find a different perspective. A mindset coach is a perfect individual for this. A mindset coach will tell someone what they need to hear and not what they want to hear while coming from a place of total objectivity.

As a mindset coach, it will be your job to provide a clear-cut reflection of a client's weaknesses. You will also highlight their strengths, so they know precisely where they stand. This will give them an honest picture of who they are and increase their self-awareness. In turn, they will become more accountable for their situation.

Self-awareness will provide a major boost in motivation. As a result, these self-aware people will seek out healthier relationships, and this will provide them with an even more positive environment. These benefits of self-awareness also lead to higher productivity and much more vibrant life.

Through all of these changes, a person will develop a healthier mindset and a reduction in stress and anxiety. Building self-awareness is vital for self-growth.

Creating Accountability

As a mindset coach, you will come into contact with clients who lack responsibility. They ignore their duties in life and seem to have no determination. As a result, life seems to be passing them by. Why do they act in this manner? Because they have no accountability and take no responsibility for their lives. These individuals often become perpetual victims in society who blame everyone else for their issues. By being their coach, you will help change their mindset, so they start having accountability for their own lives.

Accountability is a necessity for a strong mindset. A mindset coach needs to be honest with their clients and let them know they own the responsibility for their actions. Whether the results are good or bad, they own them. Once the client realizes this, they will start making more rational decisions because they know the heat will fall on them ultimately.

Of course, all of this is easier said than done. Building account-ability takes a while. It will not happen overnight or with one good pep talk. If a person has been avoiding responsibility all their lives, it will take time for them to come to terms with being accountable. Building accountability takes a lot of motiva-tion, which we will discuss in the next section.

Increasing Motivation

This goes beyond opening a book of motivational quotes and regurgitating them all. At most, these will provide short-term motivation that will likely dissipate after one session. The goal is to rewire the mind and change the way a client thinks. This will lead to results that are authentic and sustainable. The client must determine their own hows and why of living their life.

As a mindset coach, you must make a client find their inner drive. From here, they will learn to thrive, and not just survive, in their work and life. Help them discover their intrinsic values and even modify them if needed. The ultimate goal here is to help your clients become someone who always gets results. They will live up to their real potential.

Setting Realistic Goals

Without solid goals, we would all be wandering aimlessly through life. Unless that is somehow a person's goal, they have some work to do. Goal setting does not come easy to many people and there can be many reasons for it, like being unmoti-vated or overwhelmed, underestimating themselves, or being stuck in a dilemma. They may also be too close to a situation to determine if a goal is achievable or not.

A mindset coach will make the goal-setting journey more manageable. The coach will guide someone towards the right path while this client determines their true goals. As they both go along, the coach will ensure their client remains on the correct path to prevent their mind from wandering all over the place. When an individual is focused, they have a better chance of achieving their selected goals.

An increased focus will lead to a stronger mindset. From here, they will be able to avoid distractions.

Boosting Self-Reflection

People fail to reflect on their lives. This is why so many people do not learn from their mistakes. They do not perform an honest reflection of their successes and failures to see where they can improve in the future. Life is a constant process of struggle, and when a person is able to overcome, that is when success is achieved. The mindset coach can help a client reflect on their goals, as well as the journey to get there.

After a client achieves their desired goals, the coach can help draft new ones. When one mountain has been climbed, another one still exists. Life is a constant journey of self-improvement, and a mindset coach plays a big role in this.

With all of these benefits of mindset coaching, it won't be difficult to convince clients that they need your help. At least, not the ones who are willing to change. You can help them in this process, as well, but in the end, they will decide when you are needed.

THE END OF A SESSION

You need to make sure every session you go through with a client is valuable. While you will make more breakthroughs on some days way more than others, you want to make progress every day. This is an hour that you and your client will never get back. Furthermore, an excellent session can turn into an excellent week, month, or year, etc. Avoid getting frustrated because even a little progress is still progress.

To summarize, the following are some of the objectives you should aim to achieve with your coaching sessions. It may take a bit of time, but as long as you are moving in the right direction, that is what matters most.

- Clarity so they are not hiding from the truth.
- A mindset that claims the client's true desires.
- A clear vision that is exciting for your client. Fear, stress, and anxiety will slowly vanquish.
- Transformation tools that your client can use every day. Remember, what your clients do outside of the

sessions are just as important as the sessions themselves.

- Realization of their self-worth.
- Overcoming procrastination and resistance to change.
- Focusing on the positive without complaining. No more making excuses.
- Having clarity on goals.
- Development of consistent habits to get closer to dreams.
- Feeling motivated, having fun, being inspired, and showing confidence.
- Being able to visualize the big picture.
- Allowing your thoughts to roam free and no longer be locked in a cage—essentially, not living with limitations.

9

BUSINESS COACHING

S o, you are finally tired of working for a boss that does not appreciate you or pay you fairly for your labor. You decide to leave and start your own business. Congratulations! You became inspired by all of the entrepreneurs around you who made their own way and built a sustainable enterprise. Whether it's the large corporation downtown, your favorite restaurant to frequent on weekends, or the laundromat around the corner, someone worked hard to open these businesses to provide a service for the general public.

With the advent of the internet and the constant improvements in technology, online and remote business ventures have also sprouted up. In fact, these have become more profitable and practical than old school brick-and-mortar shops of the past. Many physical businesses are even transitioning to remote and online functionalities. These changes have resulted in many more entrepreneurs sprouting up, leading to more financially independent people. On the flip side, it has led to more business failures, as well.

There are many misconceptions out there about business. This is because people see the end results, and not all of the struggles that happened beforehand. In addition, they do not realize the issues that continue to exist for business owners, many of whom are hanging on by a thread. When these individuals become inspired, they move forward without much preparation. Maybe they received advice from a few business owners, read a few books, and attended some seminars, but they did not do all of the necessary legwork to help make the business sustainable. This is why so many businesses close their doors within the first year.

Before a person even considers opening a business of any kind, they must do proper research, including market trends, how they can help the public, marketing options, budgeting, and of course, a business plan. There are many moving parts, so it can be impossible to take everything into account. If someone is lucky, they can find a business mentor to guide them. Others look towards family and friends for advice, but as we have established already, they are not the most reliable source for unbiased information. In fact, many of them may try to talk you out of it and stay on the safe route. The last thing you want when trying to start a business is for someone to take away your motivation.

Another great option is to hire a business coach. A business coach typically has a background in business and uses their knowledge and experience to guide others in their entrepreneurial ventures. While there is plenty of information online and a wealth of business books available, it is all very generic and not targeted towards your specific business, which will have its own challenges.

Business coaches are able to provide a more personalized approach, which many future business owners will benefit from. In addition, they can hold people accountable for performing the necessary steps and not taking shortcuts. While people can read about the action steps they need to perform, it does not mean they will do them. It is human nature to find an easier way, and this will lead to skipping over critical tasks. Suddenly, the easier way turns into the hard way. A business coach can help ensure their clients stay on track and don't try to skip ahead.

A business coach will work alongside their clients through every process they are needed. This includes the planning phase, startup, and actually running the business. Once again, a business coach will not give direct answers or advice, but will help a business person navigate through rough waters in order to find their own solutions. Just like if you're on a sports team, you will have someone in your corner. This will lead to less stress and worry, which is a priceless benefit in and of itself.

YOU AS A BUSINESS COACH

If you have a background in business and want to enter the life coaching field, business coaching might be right up your alley. If you do not have a business background yet, you can develop these skills as a general life coach and then transition into business coaching. While you are growing your life coaching clients, you will learn several strategies and techniques of entrepreneurship, and these will serve you very well.

The focus of this section will be to discuss your role as a business coach and how you can help your clients with their success. You will serve as both a trainer and a mentor. You will be by your client's side to serve as a valuable source for information. Your clients will need help refining their talents, assessing and narrowing their goals, guiding their decisions, big and small, and doing whatever is needed to help their business succeed.

Right from the start, whenever your client hires you, your role will be as a guiding light every step of the way. The best-case scenario is that your client hires you at the beginning, from the moment they think about starting a business. That way, you can help them with the whole pre-planning, initiation, growth, and continued success phases.

At the start, you must learn everything you can about your client's company so that you are going in without any major surprises. Understand the value of the brand, the target customers, and the many challenges they are facing and will run into down the line. Whatever information you can gather will make your job much easier.

Once you have learned what the company has to offer, it's time to learn about their vision. What do they see for themselves in the future, including short- and long-term goals? Are they expecting to grow the company, or keep it a small operation? Make sure you get clear goals from your client. If they don't have any, you need to sit down with them and figure out what they are.

Every business owner will have a unique vision for their company. This is where business coaching can become more valuable than any book or seminar. You will be able to provide personalized attention based on the vision your client has.

After having all of this initial information, you can now help your client come up with beneficial and attainable goals. Take into account their current finances, time availability, motivation, and other resources. These goals will ultimately work towards fulfilling the vision that was created earlier. Once these goals are set, then it's time to take action. You will assist your client in meeting their desired goals by coming up with a set of strategies and action steps. These strategies will also help navigate through challenges and unforeseen circumstances.

Running a business, whether small or large, is risky, challenging, and nerve-racking. Just knowing that a strong and informative support system exists will put your client at extreme ease.

As you can see, business coaches are not just there for struggling businesses. They can be the key to pushing an already successful business to the next level or helping a new business grow and prosper as seamlessly as possible.

SELLING YOURSELF AS A BUSINESS COACH

Business owners, entrepreneurs, CEOs, and other business professionals may be some of the hardest people to sell to. New or prospective business owners will be squeezing every penny and will not want to hire a coach that will cost more of an investment. CEOs and other heads of large corporations are highly suspicious of people they don't know and might be resistant to your coaching services. They will probably not see the value at first.

As a business coach, it is your job to show others that you are valuable. On top of having a good marketing strategy, you have to show your potential clients that the benefits you provide will heavily outweigh the cost to hire you. Even though that's your goal, they may not know that. They may see you as a swindler.

When you are pitching your services, you will need to provide the many benefits of working with a life coach. The following are some of the best reasons to give them.

Taking More, Better, and Smarter Actions

People will do exactly what they want to do in the end. A business coach will be able to work with a client to determine exactly what they want for themselves and their business. Once a business person creates an ideal goal, they are much more likely to take consistent action to reach it. In essence, they will be taking more, better, and smarter actions because they have a goal they truly want. Having clear goals in business is imperative; otherwise, you will have no idea when your business is succeeding or failing.

Having a More Balanced Life

Having it all means that you have a balanced life. This can be very difficult to achieve because a business does take up so much of your time. A businessperson must learn to be selfish. This is different from egotistical. A good business coach will show their clients exactly how to be selfish, yet still responsible, so they get their needs met and are still liked by people. The client will design their ideal life of balance between business, home, health, and self-care.

Keeping and Making More Money

Of course, the main reason to go into business is to make a profit. The money is where it's at. You deserve to keep more of your money because you worked hard to build your business. A business coach will help you set up a plan to bring in more profits. In addition, they will help you with a financial plan and help design a strategy to earn more from your business. You will also get more customers. This benefit alone will be worth the investment in a business coach. As a coach yourself, you should probably provide a summary of how you can help the client's business thrive.

They Will Reach for More

A business coach is a partner. When someone has a partner they trust, they will reach for more because they can afford to. While reaching for more, the business person will not be consumed in the process.

Make Better Decisions Due to Better Focus

A good business coach knows the value of sharing ideas with someone who understands them. They are subjective enough to want more for their clients, but objective enough to not be biased in their approach. At the very least, a business coach can be an unbiased listening ear who can hear what their client has to say. Sometimes, just talking to someone who doesn't show judgment is enough to make ideas become more clear.

Having More Sustainable Energy

When a business person has fewer problems and more solutions, they will have more energy too. This will increase their productivity and outcomes, as well. When working with a coach, the business owner will also know they have a backup.

THE BIGGEST OBSTACLES FOR SUCCESSFUL BUSINESS COACHING

As a business coach, you will be an entrepreneur yourself. You will need to market, set up a business plan, watch your finances, pay taxes, and deal with the other challenges that come with running a business. This field of coaching is very rewarding, but it also comes with its share of obstacles. If you want to become successful in this field, you must be aware of these challenges and how to overcome them. The following list was from a survey done on those who wanted to become business coaches in the future.

Lack of Confidence/Fear of Failure

Lack of confidence was the number one response that individuals give as their biggest obstacle towards becoming a successful business coach. Many were concerned when it came to coaching high-level executives. They worried about how they could pull it off and not look like a fraud. They also wondered what would happen if they were put in this situation and they failed. Would their coaching business come to a screeching halt?

One thing to understand is that being a business coach does not mean you know the ins and outs of every business. That would be impossible. Being a business coach involves having the right coaching strategies and the ability to ask thoughtful and purposeful questions. This means that your coach training is essential for helping you develop your techniques and style so you can help other people in their circumstances.

Remember one more thing: As the coach, you are not giving any business professionals the answers. They are coming up with their own solutions. Your role is to guide them as needed. So, don't worry that you are not as experienced as the high-level executive at a Fortune 500 company or that you haven't owned a restaurant for 20 years. Running the business is their role; coaching is yours.

Finally, you are a business owner as a life coach. You had to develop specific strategies, and if they are good enough to attract major clients, you must be doing something right. Use these wins as inspiration. You can definitely handle it.

Lack of Business Skills

I addressed this a little bit in the previous section, but many inspiring coaches feel like they don't have adequate business skills. Here are some of the concerns:

- Whether the business experience they have is relevant or not.

- They know how to succeed themselves, but are unsure if they can coach others to do the same.
- They fear their lack of knowledge in areas of sales, finance, the tech industry, or any other field they might come across.

Well, it's good that you are a little worried. This shows that you care about helping others and are not overconfident. The solution here is to appreciate the integrity you possess and make sure to never lose it. Here are a few more things to consider:

- You will learn how relevant your business skills are once you start coaching clients.
- Coach training will show you how to coach others. Your goal is not to learn about every industry that exists in the world. Your goal is to learn how to coach anyone from any industry in the world.
- Coaching skills like communication, team-building, controlling emotions, and asking appropriate questions can be applied to any context.

The issue of lacking business skills will begin to resolve when you start moving forward. Don't allow this fear to stop you because many business owners can benefit from your skillset.

Lack of Resources

Resources generally refer to time and proper connections. Money can cover the costs of a startup. If you don't have certain skills, like website design, then you can hire someone to do it for you. If you have the right connections, you can find clients much more easily. All of this is true. You do need some money and connections to build a new business, including a coaching business.

How much do you need? Surprisingly, not very much. The most important aspect of a coaching practice is the message that you bring. This will heavily make up for any lack of resources you have. Pay more attention to sending out the right message than having a lack of proper resources. Those can definitely be gained.

Time Management

Time management is definitely a crucial element in starting any business. Time is something you will never get back, so you must use it wisely. A common misconception related to time is how long it takes to get things done. Becoming a full-fledged business coach from start to finish can take a long time. This is especially true when you take into account marketing and building up your clientele. Don't believe that you will start training tomorrow and then have a successful practice within a couple of weeks. It does not work that way.

I want you to consider something. The time will pass anyway, so use it to build up your skills and business load. If you stick with it, you will make continuous progress and still become a business coach in a reasonable amount of time. Set timelines for yourself to complete certain milestones. For example, you will have gone through coach training within one month from now, have a functioning website a week after the training is complete, and begin marketing the following week. Stick to these timelines as much as possible.

Procrastination

Who doesn't procrastinate these days? Way too many people do, and this is the enemy of productivity. If you procrastinate when trying to build up your coaching practice, you will deny yourself the success you can obtain. In some cases, it can ruin your business as a whole. Imagine having clients and not attending to their needs because you are procrastinating. Your clients won't appreciate it, and you will not develop a good name. We suggest setting up a weekly calendar of goals you want to achieve and sticking to them religiously. In addition, take some training on overcoming procrastination if you feel this is an issue for you.

When work needs to get done, start on it as soon as possible. If something is due in five days, work on it daily so you are not overly stressed and rushing on the fifth day. When you are rushed, simple errors get made, and they add up to be a lot.

All of these obstacles can be overcome. Never let them, or any others, stop you from living your dream as a business coach.

BUILDING TRUST

We have spoken throughout this book about the need to build trust. A relationship between a coach and their client is all about trust. If it does not exist, progress will never be made. A client will never open up about their issues, and the interaction will become pointless.

No matter what type of business you are in, your client and customers must have faith that you have their best interest at heart. They cannot feel like you're taking advantage of them in some way. It certainly cannot come across like you want to take their money. Remember, building trust can take a while and be lost in an instant. However, when you build trust, it will pay off immensely.

Life coaching is all about building trust and this section will go over some habits that will help you earn it. The key word is 'earn.'

Figure Out What Integrity Means to You

Believe it or not, not everyone agrees on what's right or wrong. We have the major issues that are accepted across the board, like it's wrong to kill, steal, or intentionally harm others. Even with these, you can get into some gray areas where people will disagree. You must determine what your core values are and stick to them. One of these values should be integrity, which means being honest and having strong moral principles. Your integrity must guide every interaction you have with a client. Check in with yourself every day and determine if you are conducting yourself with honesty and have the client's best intentions in mind.

Give Your Clients Peace of Mind

Your clients should always feel like you are taking good care of them. You don't have to be perfect, but you should always give everything you have. Despite how you are feeling, you should give your clients the best service you can. They rely on you and deserve the best of you.

Truthfully, if you are in a coaching session and your mind is wandering, you are doing your clients a huge disservice. They are there to have you listen to them, and you are there to help them find solutions. No matter what is going on, show up and give it your all.

Keep Your Word

You're probably saying 'duh,' but this is something that must be addressed. If you make a promise, then keep it. Clients have come to expect a lack of follow-through from many businesses today. Do not allow this to happen in your coaching practice. You are dealing with people in some of their most vulnerable times, and they rely on you to keep your word.

This goes for small promises, as well. Don't ever assume that because the promise you made was insignificant, you can just not follow up on it. First of all, it might be significant to your client, and they will resent you for not taking it seriously. Second, if you break a promise, it will slowly become a habit. So, don't ever start.

Schedule Some Time for Nurturing

Schedule a little additional time when you can to further develop a client relationship. Meet somewhere outside of a regular coaching session. For example, meet up for coffee, have an extra phone conversation, or buy them a small gift. It doesn't have to be anything lavish. Just let them know you value the coach-client relationship. Make them feel special. This will provide them more encouragement to follow through on action steps.

Be Upfront With Them About What You Offer

The client must have a clear understanding of what services you actually provide. Never advertise a service you cannot deliver on. If you feel you cannot offer the client what they need, like therapy or more advanced techniques you are not trained for, then be upfront with them. They will always appreciate your honesty.

Keep Things Consistent

Your clients will always expect the best level of care, so give it to them. Make sure you are living up to your commitment with each interaction.

Don't Fake Authenticity

Clients will be able to see through a facade. Maybe not right away, but eventually, they will. You cannot fake authenticity. You must genuinely care for your clients and want to help them. Let your real personality shine through and allow them to fall in love with it. As a coach, you are selling yourself too, after all.

Face-to-Face When You Can

We realize you will have clients from all over the world. Also, there will be many other reasons why face-to-face interactions will not always be possible. However, when they are, make it happen. This will allow for a stronger connection between a coach and client. Furthermore, if you are doing a remote session, opt for a video call over a regular phone call.

Don't Abandon Your Clients for New Ones

As you gain more clients when your business begins to thrive, do not sacrifice the service you have been giving to your old clients. They have been loyal and still rely on your help. Never abandon them for new clients. If you ever get to the point where you are too overwhelmed, then avoid bringing in anyone new until you can get more settled.

When You Mess Up, Own It and Fix It

When you screw something up, will you feel foolish? Probably. Will you look foolish? Most likely. Do you know what's worse than being a screw-up? Being a liar. Therefore, when you make a mistake, own it and fix it. Don't try to hide it. We are all humans and make mistakes. Your clients will appreciate your honesty more than they care about you messing up. Just make sure you are not making the same mistakes over and over again.

You are on your way to becoming a highly successful business coach. If this area does not tickle your fancy, other coaching options exist too.

CONCLUSION

All of us at Elvin Coaches want to thank you for taking the time to read our book, *Don't Make Me Use My Life Coach Voice*. We hope that it painted a detailed portrait of what a life coach is and the value they can bring to the people who need them. Life coaching is definitely a growing field with many different offshoots. Every type of coaching subset has its own unique methods that work for them. For example, intuitive coaching, mindset coaching, and business coaching, all of which we covered, can benefit from their separate techniques. At the same time, the core principles of the coaching field can be used across the spectrum.

As we went through the different parts of the book, we provided the foundations of what life coaching is, the benefits the practice provides, common misconceptions, and reasons why you, the reader, should consider this as a profession. While the monetary gains can be abundant once you become good at your craft, the true value in life coaching rests in how many people from all walks of life can be touched by your special gifts. Literally anyone can benefit from life coaching, which was demonstrated by the number of different styles and techniques we went over, plus the variety of high-profile individuals who have used and praised life coaches.

Habit formation is another main topic that was covered in this book. Improving your circumstances is all about changing your habits, or daily routines and rituals. What you think and do on a daily basis determines the outcomes you will ultimately get. Therefore, a major focus of any coach-client relationship needs to be that of creating and reforming habits. When a client learns these techniques, they can positively change any area of their lives.

A life coach can literally help a person in every aspect of their life, including career, health, spirituality, and relationships. Some coaches choose to become specialized, while others stay more general. One thing a life coach is not, no matter what kind, is a therapist. They do not deal with mental health disorders, or anything of that nature. Their goal is to focus on the present and build towards a better future for their clients.

Another foundational principle with life coaching is that they don't give people answers. They are more focused on asking the right questions and helping their clients come up with their own solutions. Think of life coaching as a guiding light.

The client must do their own walking, climbing, digging, swimming, or whatever else to get to their desired destination.

While we provided a series of questions to ask your clients, as you gain experience, you will come up with many of your own. You will also become more aware of when and how to ask questions, which is equally important.

ARE YOU READY?

As a life coach, you will have the capability to change people's lives in ways you cannot imagine. An individual will look at life so differently after they have benefited from some good coaching session. While coaches are not miracle workers, they can help alter a person's reality, so a life they thought was once unattainable will now be something they actively work towards. The profession is difficult. There will be many challenges and a rollercoaster of emotions. However, the value it brings to clients is completely worth it. To watch someone who was once broken down rise up and face the world is an indescribable experience.

If you are ready to pursue this path, we urge you to take the information in this book and begin practicing it faithfully. We feel this book will serve as a great launching point for anyone who wants to become a life coach. At Elvin Coaches, we take our passion for being great coaches very seriously. Therefore, we are here to provide you support along your journey, as we want to build as many wonderful life coaches as possible.

We want to help as many people as possible with this information. If you found value in this book, please leave a review online so more people can become aware of it. Thank you again, and best of luck to you on your journey. We have faith in you!

Finally, if you did enjoy this book, we are about to make you much happier. This book is the first in what will be a series of similar topics. Our next book will be available soon in an advanced version to cover some of the sub-niche options in life coaching.

Just for you!

A FREE GIFT TO OUR READERS

Scan the QR code to subscribe or follow the link
https://elvinlifecoaches.activehosted.com/f/3

You're going to receive the

Wheel of Life Coaching Technique

and other goodies

REFERENCES

Adams, B. (2017, September 7). *6 Morning Rituals of Steve Jobs, Tony Robbins, Oprah, and Other Successful Leaders.* Inc.Com. https://www.inc.com/bryan-adams/6-celebrity-morning-rituals-to-help-you-kick-ass.html

Altmann, G. (n.d.). *Success Text.* Retrieved September 10, 2020, from https://www.pexels.com/photo/marketing-school-business-idea-21696/

Andrews, A. (n.d.). *Full Moon Illustration.* Retrieved September 9, 2020, from https://www.pexels.com/photo/full-moon-illustration-861443/

Arya, N. (n.d.). *Photography of Book Page.* Retrieved September 9, 2020, from https://www.pexels.com/photo/photography-of-book-page-1029141/

Autocratic. (n.d.). Coachingsportleadership.Weebly.Com. Retrieved September 4, 2020, from https://coachingsportleadership.weebly.com/autocratic.html#:~:text=The%20Autocratic%20coach%20takes%20on

Bertolazzi, I. (n.d.), *Neon Signage.* Retrieved September 10, 2020, from https://www.pexels.com/photo/neon-signage-2681319/

Blackbyrn, S. (2018, March 19). *Types of Coaching Styles And Models Every Coach Should Know About.* ..Coach; .Coach Blog. https://sai.coach/blog/types-of-coaching-styles/

Blackbyrn, S. (2019, December 30). *How To Become A Successful Mindset Coach: Convincing Clients Made Easy! - .Coach.* ..Coach; .Coach Blog. https://sai.coach/blog/how-to-become-a-successful-mindset-coach/

Bonham-Carter, D. (2007). *Life Coaching for Problem Habits - A Model for Life Coaches.* www.Davidbonham-Carter.Com. http://www.davidbonham-carter.com/article-modelofchange.html

Bundrant, M. (n.d.). *Top Five Obstacles To Becoming A Successful Business Coach And Their Solutions (Survey Results)» INLP Center.* INLP Center. Retrieved September 10, 2020, from https://inlpcenter.org/obstacles-for-business-coaches/

Casano, T. (2016, March 24). *11 Celebrities Who Prove Using A Life Coach Will Help Reboot Your Career*. Elite Daily. https://www.elitedaily.com/entertainment/celebrities-life-coach-career/1426180

Cesario, A. (n.d.). *Opened Glass Window*. Retrieved September 9, 2020, from https://www.pexels.com/photo/opened-glass-window-1906795/

Clear, J. (2018, July 13). *James Clear*. James Clear. https://jamesclear.com/new-habit

Colleen-Joy. (2018, May 18). *My top 20 Life Coaching Questions*. InnerLifeSkills. https://www.innerlifeskills.com/life-coaching-tools/my-top-20-coaching-questions/

Cook, C. (n.d.). *Photo of Blue Doorway*. Retrieved September 9, 2020, from https://www.pexels.com/photo/photo-of-blue-doorway-2929910/

C.S. Lewis Quote: Integrity is doing the right thing even when no one is watching. | Goalcast. (2018). Goalcast. https://www.goalcast.com/2018/03/26/15-c-s-lewis-quotes/c-s-lewis-quote1/

Davis, S. (n.d.). *Aircrafts Flying and Leaving Contrail*. Retrieved September 2, 2020, from https://www.pexels.com/photo/aircrafts-flying-and-leaving-contrail-4400026/

Elsey, E.-L. (2019, February 20). *10 of My All-Time Best Coaching Questions & Why! | The Launchpad - The*

Coaching Tools Company Blog. The Coaching Tools Company. https://www.thecoachingtoolscompany.com/10-time-best-coaching-questions/

Fauxels. (n.d.). *Man and Woman Near Table.* Retrieved September 9, 2020, from https://www.pexels.com/photo/man-and-woman-near-table-3184465/

Gavin de Becker Quotes (Author of The Gift of Fear). (n.d.). Www.Goodreads.Com. Retrieved September 5, 2020, from https://www.goodreads.com/author/quotes/31933.Gavin_de_Becker

Greater Minds. (n.d.-b). *What Is The Law Of Attraction? And How To Use It Effectively.* The Law Of Attraction. Retrieved September 1, 2020, from https://www.thelawofattraction.com/what-is-the-law-of-attraction/

Grushnikov, A. (n.d.). *Black and White Photos of Clocks.* Retrieved September 9, 2020, from https://www.pexels.com/photo/black-and-white-photo-of-clocks-707676/

Inner Glow Circle. (2019). What is Life Coaching and What Do Life Coaches Do?! (The Truth About Life Coaching) [YouTube Video]. In *YouTube.* https://www.youtube.com/watch?v=Ma1UWKLHrYQ&t=4s

Khan, S. (2019, July 13). *Six Benefits Of Working With A Business Coach.* Entrepreneur. https://www.entrepreneur.com/article/336762

Krasnow, P. (2018, April 18). *15 Habits for Earning Your Clients' Trust*. Outpost Blog. https://www.teamoutpost.com/blog/earning-clients-trust/

Ledwell, N. (n.d.). *HOW TO CHANGE YOUR BAD HABITS | Authentic Me | Nicky Massyn Life Coaching - Confidence, Well-being, Fertility Mindset - South West London*. Authentic Me. Retrieved September 9, 2020, from https://nickymassyn-lifecoach.com/blog/2019/3/15/how-to-change-your-bad-habits

Life Coach Insights: 3 Simple Strategies for Changing Habits. (2016, January 1). Jody Michael Associates. https://www.jodymichael.com/blog/3-simple-strategies-for-changing-habits/

Life Purpose Institute Admin. (2016, June 7). *7 Reasons To Become A Life Coach*. Life Purpose Institute. https://www.lifepurposeinstitute.com/7-reasons-to-become-a-life-coach/

Lonczak, H. (2020, April 16). *What's Your Coaching Approach? 10 Different Coaching Styles Explained*. Positive-Psychology.Com. https://positivepsychology.com/coaching-styles/#:~:text=It%20is%20a%20solution%2Dfocused

Lopes, H. (n.d.). *Four Person Standing on Cliff in Front of Sun*. Retrieved September 2, 2020, from https://www.pexels.com/photo/backlit-dawn-foggy-friendship-697243

Mentatdgt. (n.d.). *Two Woman Chatting*. Retrieved September 9, 2020, from https://www.pexels.com/photo/two-woman-chatting-1311518/

Miedaner, T. (2015). *What is a Life Coach? - LifeCoach.com.* LifeCoach.Com. https://www.lifecoach.com/what-is-a-life-coach/

Milanesi, M. (n.d.). *Photo of Mountain Under Starry Night Sky*. Retrieved September 9, 2020, from https://www.pexels.com/photo/photo-of-mountain-under-starry-night-sky-2670898/

Miller, B. (2020). *The 7 Common Challenges of Coaching*. Workboard.Com. https://www.workboard.com/blog/coaching-challenges.php

Mindvalley. (n.d.). *The Ultimate Guide of Powerful Coaching Techniques*. Evercoach. Retrieved September 6, 2020, from https://www.evercoach.com/ultimate-guide-of-powerful-coaching-techniques

Negative Space. (n.d.). *Person Writing on White paper*. Retrieved September 9, 2020, from https://www.pexels.com/photo/fashion-woman-notebook-pen-34072/

Pixabay. (n.d.). *Black Android Smartphone on Top of White Book*. Retrieved September 9, 2020, from https://www.pexels.com/photo/black-android-smartphone-on-top-of-white-book-39584/

Pixabay. (n.d.-b). *Clear Glass With Red Sand Grainer.* Retrieved September 9, 2020, from https://www.pexels.com/photo/clear-glass-with-red-sand-grainer-39396/

Pixabay. (n.d.-b). *Clear Light Bulb.* Retrieved September 9, 2020, from https://www.pexels.com/photo/abstract-blackboard-bulb-chalk-355948/

Pixabay. (n.d.-d). *Exit Signage Pointing at Right Side.* Retrieved September 9, 2020, from https://www.pexels.com/photo/arrow-communication-direction-display-235975/

Pixabay. (n.d.-d). *Human Fist.* Retrieved September 9, 2020, from https://www.pexels.com/photo/human-fist-163431/

Pixabay. (n.d.-f). *Pile of Rock Near Lake.* Retrieved September 9, 2020, from https://www.pexels.com/photo/balance-blur-boulder-close-up-355863/

Pixabay. (n.d.-g). *Question Mark illustration.* Retrieved September 9, 2020, from https://www.pexels.com/photo/ask-blackboard-chalk-board-chalkboard-356079/

Ratan Tata Quote: "None can destroy iron, but its own rust can! Likewise none can destroy a person, but its own mindset can!" (n.d.). Quotefancy.Com. Retrieved September 10, 2020, from https://quotefancy.com/quote/1439955/Ratan-Tata-None-can-destroy-iron-but-its-own-rust-can-Likewise-none-can-destroy-a-person

Roseplay, D. (n.d.). *Wooden Stamp on Ink Pad Placed on Desk*. Retrieved September 9, 2020, from https://www.pexels.com/photo/wooden-stamp-on-ink-pad-placed-on-desk-3839649/

Stewart, J. (2014). *Top Ten Myths About Life Coaching*. www.Schoolofcoachingmastery.Com. https://www.schoolofcoachingmastery.com/coaching-blog/top-ten-myths-about-life-coaching

The Coaching Academy Blog. (n.d.). *9 Key Ideas to Build and Change Your Habits | Blog | The Coaching Academy*. Www.the-Coaching-Academy.Com. Retrieved September 9, 2020, from https://www.the-coaching-academy.com/blog/9-key-ideas-to-build-and-change-your-habits-3185.asp

The Complete Guide to Intuitive Life Coaching. (n.d.). Life Coach Spotter. Retrieved September 6, 2020, from https://www.lifecoachspotter.com/intuitive-life-coach/#expectfrom

Tracy, B. (2018, August 17). *Business Coaching: A Guide to Everything You Need to Know | Brian...* Brian Tracy's Self Improvement & Professional Development Blog. https://www.briantracy.com/blog/business-success/business-coaching/

What is a Life Coach? Learn What Does a Life Coach Do To Help You. (2016). Tonyrobbins.Com. https://www.tonyrobbins.com/coaching/results-life-coach/

Wilson, G. (n.d.). *What are coaching styles and how do they work?* Www.Thesuccessfactory.Co.Uk. Retrieved September 7, 2020, from https://www.thesuccessfactory.co.uk/blog/coaching-styles-and-how-they-work

Winget, L. (2012, July 13). *Stop settling for average!* Larry Winget. https://www.larrywinget.com/stop-settling-for-average/

Weinschenk, S. (2019, April 19). *The Science of Habits*. Psychology Today. https://www.psychologytoday.com/gb/blog/brain-wise/201904/the-science-habits

Made in the USA
Las Vegas, NV
04 November 2023

80237660R00100